MATTERS OF LIFE AND DEATH

About the Author

Stephanie O'Connor is the winner of the 2025 Hubert Butler Essay Prize. Her writing examines ethical and legal questions in healthcare and public life, with particular attention to moral agency, research, practices of care, and responsibility.

HAUS CURIOSITIES

MATTERS OF LIFE AND DEATH

Moral Responsibility, Care, and Dignity in Dying

Stephanie O'Connor

First published by Haus Publishing in 2026
4 Cinnamon Row
London SW11 3TW
www.hauspublishing.com

A CIP catalogue record for this book is available from the British Library

ISBN: 978-1-914979-55-2
eISBN: 978-1-914979-56-9

Typeset in Garamond by MacGuru Ltd

Printed in Czechia

All paper products used in the production of this book are FSC certified and acquired from sustainable sources.

The authorised representative in the EEA is:
Haus Publishing, Casella Postale 32
50037 San Piero a Sieve (Fi), Italy
gpsr@hauspublishing.com

Contents

Introduction

'Men must endure
Their going hence, even as their coming hither.'
—William Shakespeare, *King Lear* (Act V, Scene ii)

A woman I knew well, a nurse by training, had spent many years working in hospital wards. Practical and attentive, she was rarely inclined toward drama.

When she received her diagnosis, aged fifty-six, she asked her questions quietly, almost courteously, as though mindful of the burden placed on those who answered them. She retained the habits of her profession even when she became the patient, listening carefully, thanking people who did not expect to be thanked. Humour became her way of carrying the worry she felt for friends, family, and those around her, and we quickly learned to read in that humour both courage and fear.

The night she died, the house filled slowly. People moved in and out, drinking tea, offering words, touching shoulders. There was a moment when someone asked whether more could have been done; another answered that there was always something more, though whether it should be was another matter.

That distinction, between what *can* be done and what *should* be done, has stayed with me. And it was thinking of her, and of others whom I have loved and lost over the years, that returned me once again to Edgar's line to his dying father, Gloucester. Not because it offers consolation, but because it presents itself as something like instruction: a form of wisdom we are meant to accept without argument, austere, inevitable, and faintly chilling. It suggests that endurance is not merely necessary but expected, and that birth and death belong to a realm beyond intervention, beyond responsibility even, to a realm in which helplessness is not only unavoidable but somehow dignified. And yet the conditions under which we meet death today have changed.

For much of human history, death was shaped by circumstance, custom, and human presence. Today, it is increasingly mediated by medicine, law, and a language of choice that suggests not only that we may intervene, but that we must decide when and how to do so.

Now, in many contemporary settings shaped by intensive care and life-sustaining technologies, we do more than witness the edges of life: we intervene, prolong, withhold, and decide, often in ways that carry responsibilities earlier generations could scarcely have imagined. What once appeared as fate now unfolds within systems of care, law, and clinical judgement that distribute responsibility across many hands. Yet our older language has not kept pace. We still speak of 'letting go' and of 'letting nature take its course', even as dying is increasingly shaped by clinical decisions, legal frameworks, personal choices, and institutional pressures. The language of inevitability lingers, not because it fits, but because it once did.

Endurance has not disappeared, but it is being recast, now entangled with decisions about when to intervene, when to withdraw, how long to continue, and who carries the weight of those decisions. The edges of life are no longer silent thresholds but crowded, contested spaces where care, law, conscience, and choice meet under conditions that are rarely clear or neutral.

*

Before I wrote the essay that led to this book,[1] I was already absorbed by healthcare ethics and the ordinary, unglamorous, yet fascinating work of trying to decide what ought to be done when the facts are incomplete, pressures real, stakes intimate, resources limited, and consequences irreversible. That attention was shaped not only by years of research-ethics committee work, but also through a long familiarity with hospitals themselves: by the slow rhythm of dependency – waiting, watching, advocating, trusting – and by observing the ethical pressures present in places where care is negotiated daily, often under considerable strain. Those years did not give me certainty; they showed me how easily moral difficulty in institutional life can be disguised as procedure.

From the outside, healthcare ethics can often appear quite administrative, with its application forms, approvals, documentation, and compliance. Yet what appears orderly may sometimes conceal moral residue that has nowhere to go. A signature may secure consent without securing actual understanding. Legal safeguards may coexist with harm. Institutional processes can give the impression that moral questions have been settled when, in truth, they have only been managed. Above all, such work reveals, as Manfred Kets de Vries observes, that vulnerability is not an exception to the human condition but one of its defining features.[2] Nowhere is this more visible than in healthcare, where dependence is not a failure of agency but a fact of life.

Over time, my attention turned increasingly to end-of-life decisions. It is here, to my mind, that many of our assumptions about autonomy, choice, and control are tested most severely. Choice matters profoundly, but it may not always bear what we ask of it. At the limits of life, illness narrows possibilities; agency is often compromised, and decisions are shaped by pain, fear, exhaustion, dependence, and unequal distributions of knowledge and power. The language of autonomy remains indispensable, but it may not be sufficient to account for the conditions under which such decisions are made, or for the responsibilities that extend beyond them – responsibilities that do not disappear, but settle, often uneasily, on those who remain.

It was from this recognition that this book began to take shape. Indeed, if it has an origin beyond the essay that preceded it, it lies in the accumulation of moments in which ethical and legal frameworks, necessary as they are, seemed unable to bear the full moral weight of what was unfolding.

The uneasy gap between what can be done and what should be done rarely announces itself dramatically. More often it emerges quietly, in incremental decisions that feel defensible yet unsettled, necessary yet incomplete. It is in these moments that judgement is most heavily felt, and least securely grounded.

Again and again, I found myself returning to a

question that does not fit easily into legal categories: not simply 'is this allowed?' but 'what is owed?'

This question first took shape in an earlier essay, but it is taken up again here in a wider and more demanding context. This book is an attempt to understand how dignity and responsibility are reshaped when dying is no longer simply endured, but increasingly directed by medicine, law, and shared decision-making.

Ireland's recent history brings this question into sharp focus. The constitutional crisis surrounding *Attorney General v X*[3] exposed the strain on legal frameworks when confronted with situations of profound vulnerability, where the risks to life, autonomy, and moral judgement could not be easily separated. Two decades later, the death of Savita Halappanavar in 2012[4] not only shocked the national conscience; it exposed how law can shape clinical decision-making, influencing not only action but hesitation. It made clear that legal frameworks do not hover neutrally above practice. They enter the hospital room. They weigh on imagination and conscience. They shape what clinicians believe they may do and what they fear they will be punished for doing.

Soon after, in 2014, the case of *PP v HSE*[5] fixed itself in my mind with a kind of terrible persistence: a young woman, clinically dead, maintained on somatic support because she was pregnant, and a grieving family forced to seek judicial permission for what they experienced as the most basic human request – to let the dead be dead. This case occupies an unsettling territory where familiar categories begin to break down: patient and corpse, care and prolongation, respect and violation. It reveals how legal reasoning, though necessary, cannot readily resolve such situations, and struggles to articulate what dignity requires when a person can no longer speak, consent, or resist.

My engagement with that case led to the essay that, in turn, led to this book, and also altered how I came to see such situations. They do not simply present conflicts; they expose the limits of the frameworks brought to resolve them. They suggest that in the most harrowing situations, what appears as a clash of competing principles is often something less settled, and that encounters with moral terrain that require forms of judgement that are less secure, more interpretive, and more exposed, grounded in imagination, conscience, and care.

At the same time, Ireland was confronting broader debates about assisted dying, including the public discussions that followed Marie Fleming's case in 2013 and subsequent legislative developments.

Whatever one's position, and this is not a debate

that lends itself to easy moral confidence, it has become increasingly clear that end-of-life questions once confined to private sorrow are moving into public deliberation and democratic judgement. In October 2024, the Dáil voted to '*take note*' of recommendations from the Joint Committee on Assisted Dying.[6] The vote did not change the law or legalise assisted dying in Ireland. It did, however, mark a shift: an issue once discussed in whispers has moved into the realm of democratic possibility.

Similar debates continue elsewhere, including in the United Kingdom. I often return to several high-profile UK cases that have shaped debate on the right to die, including Tony Bland, Diane Pretty, Debbie Purdy, and Tony Nicklinson, each marking a moment when personal autonomy collided with legal restraint. At present, assisted dying remains unlawful across the UK, although patients retain the right to refuse treatment and to receive palliative care aimed at relieving suffering. Current parliamentary debate centres on whether to legalise medically assisted dying for certain terminally ill, mentally competent adults under strict safeguards, as proposed in the Terminally Ill Adults (End of Life) Bill. Whether such legislation ultimately passes or fails, the deeper point remains: this is not a passing controversy but part of a wider shift in how societies understand death, agency, care, responsibility, and dignity.

Alongside these developments, something else has begun to enter the scene more quietly. Decisions in healthcare have never been made in isolation; they have always been shaped by systems, by protocols, guidelines, institutional norms, and forms of professional judgement that extend beyond any single individual. What is changing is not the presence of such systems, but their character.

Artificial intelligence belongs to this shift. It matters not because it introduces entirely new ethical questions, but because it alters something subtler: how judgement is formed, how responsibility is distributed, and how decisions come to feel justified. Its significance lies less in what it can do than in how it reshapes our sense of who is responsible, and for what. What interests and troubles me is not novelty, but something more subdued: the promises such systems make, of clarity where ambiguity persists, of outputs where discernment is required, and of conclusions that can appear to relieve us of burden. These questions rarely announce themselves clearly. They emerge instead in ordinary situations: in a diagnosis, a recommendation, a decision about how far treatment should continue.

What follows is not an argument against such

technologies, nor an endorsement of them, but an attempt to understand how they alter the ways in which responsibility is carried, how persons are recognised, and how dignity is preserved when life approaches its end.

Across these domains – assisted dying, end-of-life law, and emerging forms of clinical decision-making – the language of choice has become dominant. Yet the presence of options does not settle the question of what is right, nor does it relieve us of the obligation to attend carefully to one another.

It is here that dignity returns, not as rhetoric, but as a discipline. I begin this book from an understanding of dignity not as ornament or slogan, but as a principle that disciplines action when circumstances are most difficult, options limited, and outcomes costly. The account of dignity developed here does not belong to any single tradition. It draws, in part, on the Kantian insistence on the irreducible worth of persons, while also attending to vulnerability, dependence, and care. It is concerned not only with respect in principle, but with what respect requires in conditions of illness, fragile agency, dependence, and constraint. On this view, dignity is relational and situational: it concerns how we respond to one another when the ability to assert one's own worth is limited or compromised.

To speak of dignity is therefore to speak of

responsibility: not merely accountability after the fact, but obligations that arise within relationships of dependence and care. End-of-life decisions are rarely borne by individuals alone. They unfold within wider frameworks that distribute their weight: among families who must live with the consequences of what they agreed to or refused; among doctors whose judgements take shape within systems of constraint; among institutions that sometimes prefer defensible procedure to morally costly discernment; and among societies that legislate not only what is permitted, but what forms of moral attention are expected.

The question is not whether suffering should be relieved, but how to do so without losing sight of those whose lives have become difficult to sustain. These are not decisions that can be absorbed entirely into systems or principles. They remain, in the end, matters of judgement, carried by those who must make them and remain answerable for what follows. At the edge of life, the distinction between freedom and responsibility begins to disappear. The questions addressed here are not abstract. They arise in situations where no position is without cost, and where that cost cannot be entirely shared. And they linger in moments where law, care, and ethical reflection meet under pressure, and where judgement must be formed without the reassurance of certainty.

The chapters that follow return to the edges of human life not to sensationalise them, but to look steadily at what they demand of us. The approach is interdisciplinary, drawing on legal cases and ethical reflection, and moving across cases, practices, and forms of reasoning. In doing so, this book does not attempt to resolve these debates definitively. Instead, it traces how such dilemmas emerge, how they are experienced, and how responsibility for them is negotiated across patients and families, clinicians and institutions, and the wider frameworks within which decisions are made.

The inquiry begins with dignity as a principle tested at the limits of life, turns to the legal and ethical tensions surrounding assisted dying, and then considers how emerging technological systems are beginning to shape judgement in care. It returns, in conclusion, to the question that runs throughout: how responsibility is to be understood and borne when decisions cannot be made cleanly, and certainty cannot be secured.

Again and again, the question returns, and cannot be deferred: not simply what is allowed, but what is owed to the dying, to those who care for them, and to the shared moral life that binds private decisions to public consequences.

If Edgar's line to his father still holds any truth

for us, it is not because we remain helpless. It is because, even now, in rooms shaped by technology, carefully worded protocols, and increasingly by systems whose judgements are not always visible, we encounter the same final fact: that there are limits to what we can control, and that control, extended far enough, begins to exact its own cost. The question that remains is not whether we can act, but how we will act – and what, in acting, we are willing to risk, to diminish, or to honour when certainty falls away.

1

Dignity at the Edge of Life

In 2014, the Irish High Court was asked to decide the case now known as *PP v HSE*. A young woman, declared clinically dead following a catastrophic event, was sustained on somatic support because she was pregnant. Around her gathered competing claims about what dignity required. Medicine could sustain biological processes; law was understood to require continuation; ethics struggled to keep pace. Her family sought the withdrawal of life-sustaining treatment, arguing that its continuation violated her dignity and inflicted further harm on them. The State, citing constitutional obligations to protect unborn life, resisted. The ventilator rendered the body biologically viable in the narrowest sense, even as meaningful life had ended.

Here, dignity was invoked by multiple parties, and for different ends. For the family, it referred to the woman's prior values, her bodily integrity, and the meaning of allowing the dead to be dead. For the State, it was bound up with constitutional protection of unborn life.

The clinicians' professional integrity was at stake; the family's grief pressed urgently for recognition. The law was required to adjudicate between these competing claims, yet the judgement could not fully resolve the moral disorientation produced by their collision.

What this case revealed was not simply a conflict of rights but a deeper ethical dislocation. Technology had begun to outpace moral consensus. Life-support systems unsettled older categories of life and death, patient and body, care and prolongation. Consent was no longer available. Benefit was contested. Responsibility was diffused.

The court ultimately permitted the withdrawal of support, but the judgment did not dissolve the unease. It could not. Law could decide what was permitted, but it could not fully answer what was owed.

Cases such as this, which recur in different forms across modern healthcare, reveal something important: dignity is both central to care and resistant to easy definition.

*

Dignity is one of the most frequently invoked terms in contemporary healthcare ethics. It appears across nursing practice, psychiatry, ageing, disability, geriatrics, palliative medicine, and end-of-life care, and many other areas of medicine. It also features in clinical guidelines, legal judgments, policy documents, and everyday public debate, often as a kind of moral seal, a word that signals seriousness without requiring much elaboration. Decisions are said to protect, promote, violate, or restore someone's dignity.

I, like so many others, have heard it spoken at the bedside, offered quietly in deeply sad moments when language begins to fail, not so much as a definition, but as a hope that something essential might still be protected. In all these ways, dignity is far from ignored. What is less consistently examined, however, is what people mean when they invoke it, and how different, sometimes incompatible understandings of dignity operate simultaneously within individual, familial, clinical, legal, and institutional settings, as we see in cases such as *PP v HSE*.

Part of the difficulty lies in the term's apparent obviousness. Much of the literature proceeds as though the meaning of dignity were self-evident, or treats it as interchangeable with related concepts such as autonomy, respect, privacy, or self-esteem.

In law and human rights discourse, 'human dignity' often denotes a basic worth belonging equally to all persons, grounding fundamental moral and political duties and rights. The 1948 Universal Declaration of Human Rights affirms the 'inherent dignity' and 'equal and inalienable rights of all members of the human family' as the 'foundation of freedom, justice and peace in the world.' In healthcare, the term is often given a more practical emphasis: the World Health Organisation, for example, describes dignity as an individual's 'inherent value and worth', linking it to respect, recognition, self-worth, and the ability to make choices. Yet historically, the term has carried very different meanings, referring variously to rank, honour, poise, integrity, and self-respect, inheritances that sit uneasily with modern appeals to dignity. With its many meanings, dignity often functions as a moral placeholder, signalling that something important is at stake without any settled account of precisely why.

This vagueness is not accidental. In reality, dignity does important work precisely because it resists easy definition. It gathers together concerns about self-worth, respect, agency, vulnerability, and treatment without collapsing them into a single narrow principle. Yet that same elasticity can make it susceptible to misuse. When dignity is treated as self-evident, there is a danger that it becomes more like a slogan than a guide. Likewise, when it is assumed rather than examined, it may obscure the very moral difficulty it is meant to illuminate. Nowhere is this tension more apparent than at the edges of life, where dignity is most frequently invoked even as agreement about its meaning grows fragile and uncertain.

Consider debates about assisted dying, for example. For some people, dignity lies in self-determination, the ability to shape the manner and timing of one's death, often in the face of suffering or loss of control. For others, dignity refers to the inherent worth of human life, irrespective of choice or mental capacity. Here, the same word anchors two opposing moral claims, each persuasive within its own framework. However, what often remains unspoken is which understanding of dignity is doing the work, who has authority to interpret it in practice, and how its invocation redistributes the responsibilities of care.

*

When we speak of dignity, we inherit a word whose history is less settled than its modern use might suggest. For much of that history, dignity did not describe equal human worth but rank, office, and recognised standing, something that could be conferred, displayed, and lost. In classical antiquity, particularly in Rome, *dignitas* referred to honour, reputation, and public office. It was not something one possessed simply by being human, but something attached to role, social standing, lineage, or achievement. Although Stoic philosophers such as Marcus Aurelius and Epictetus began to detach human worth from social rank and hierarchy, locating it instead in rational self-command, the language of dignity still retained its association with recognition and role. Senators and magistrates had dignity; slaves did not. Dignity, in this sense, was unequal, tied to decorum and self-command, and vulnerable to loss through disgrace.

Medieval Christian thought preserved this structure even as it complicated it. While all persons were said to possess spiritual worth as creatures made in the image of God (*imago Dei*), the Great Chain of Being ensured that social hierarchy persisted. Kings, clergy, and nobles bore dignity through office, while the poor, the sick, and the dependent were recipients of charity rather than bearers of equal standing. Care for the poor and the sick could be genuine and attentive, yet still shaped by hierarchy and condescension. Dignity, in this world, was preserved through order rather than equality. Traces of this still linger today wherever care risks slipping into quiet paternalism.

By the early modern period, dignity remained closely bound to honour, reputation, and self-command. It was something enacted before others: to appear undignified was to fall short of expected conduct. This forms part of the moral background to literary sources such as Shakespeare's King Lear, where endurance, suffering, and composure appear dignified, whereas complaint, exposure, or loss of control threatens public standing. Although modern ethics formally rejects these inherited hierarchies, their influence persists.

In healthcare settings, this is visible often in subtle ways wherever independence is treated as more dignified than dependence, continence more dignified than incontinence, cognitive competence more dignified than confusion, and composure more dignified than distress. Even privacy is often treated as synonymous with dignity itself. We see examples of this at the bedside, surfacing in small hesitations: a curtain drawn a little too late; a decision explained in language a patient cannot follow; a silence that says more than any policy. In this sense, dignity is often measured by how closely someone approximates the ideal autonomous adult, showing that status-based understandings of dignity still very much persist in modern form. This helps explain why severe illness, dependency, or decline are so often experienced as the loss of dignity, and how care can unintentionally demean even when well-intentioned.

Alongside these inherited meanings sit two dominant strands of modern ethical thought. One understands dignity as inherent worth, possessed equally by all human beings regardless of achievement or capacity, and is often discussed in contemporary philosophy, including Kant and modern human rights discourse. On this account, dignity cannot be earned or lost; illness, disability, and dependency do not diminish it. It exists simply by virtue of being human. Another, highly influential in contemporary bioethics, links dignity closely to autonomy, emphasising self-determination, choice, and control over one's own life and body. Respecting dignity here is understood as respecting a person's authority to decide, and has shaped practices such as informed consent, advance directives, and patient-centred care. Each captures something essential, yet there is no stable meaning across them, and neither alone resolves the tensions exposed at the end of life.

When autonomy alone becomes the primary lens through which dignity is interpreted, older status hierarchies can quietly return, re-ranking those whose agency is constrained by illness or dependency. Care then risks becoming a space where dignity appears granted or withheld rather than recognised as already present, spoken about rather than with people, and rendered most fragile precisely where moral concern should be greatest.

This is why dignity remains both indispensable and unsettled in healthcare ethics. It gathers our deepest concerns about worth and vulnerability while resisting any single, final definition.

*

Any serious discussion of dignity must reckon with the philosopher Immanuel Kant. For Kant, dignity is grounded in rational moral agency: the capacity to ask whether the principle behind one's action could be willed as universal law.[1] Human beings, he argued, possess *Würde*, or dignity, and must never be treated merely as means but always as ends in themselves. Kant's account rejects the idea that a person's worth depends on status or role, and his insistence that persons cannot be reduced to instruments of utility has been deeply influential in shaping modern bioethics and human rights discourse. It gives dignity moral depth and structure, and helps to explain why coercion and exploitation are wrong, why informed consent matters, and why a person must not be reduced merely to a case, a burden, or a problem to be managed.

Alongside this tradition sits another, also highly

influential, though differently oriented. In the work of utilitarian philosophers John Stuart Mill and Jeremy Bentham,[2] the moral focus turns toward the consequences of action, the alleviation of suffering, the promotion of well-being, and the weighing of harm and benefit. In healthcare, this orientation is visible in the balancing of burdens and benefits, in assessments of quality of life, and in efforts to minimise harm. Kant reminds us that persons must not be reduced to means; Mill and Bentham remind us that suffering matters and cannot be ignored. Both traditions have shaped contemporary bioethics, and each brings something essential into view. Yet neither, taken alone, resolves the tensions that arise at the limits of life.

If dignity is grounded primarily in rational agency, as Kant suggests, questions arise as to how it is to be understood when agency is diminished, fragmented, or absent. Severe illness, cognitive decline, dementia, and unconsciousness all challenge the assumption that autonomy is intact. Kant's insistence that persons must never be treated merely as means retains its moral force here, but it cannot by itself determine how dignity is to be understood or enacted when agency falls silent.

At the same time, if moral judgement is guided primarily by the reduction of suffering, as in utilitarian traditions, difficult questions arise about how suffering is measured, whose suffering counts, and what forms of life are worth sustaining.

This does not mean that these traditions are mistaken. Rather, it suggests that neither, taken alone, is sufficient to address the full range of moral experience at the limits of life. If dignity is to matter where agency falters, and if care is to respond adequately to suffering without reducing a person to a set of outcomes, then the moral work required exceeds what either framework can securely contain.

Modern medicine brings these tensions into sharp focus. Technologies that prolong life, relieve pain, or sustain biological function force decisions that are not easily resolved by appeal to principle or calculation alone. A person may be alive, dependent, and deeply vulnerable, yet unable to exercise the very capacities through which dignity is often said to be realised. One sees this, for example, in the patient who no longer speaks, whose breathing is assisted by a machine, while family members stand nearby trying to understand what continuing treatment now asks of them. At the same time, assessments of suffering and benefit may sit uneasily alongside intuitions about respect, restraint, and the moral significance of the person.

Of course, Kant, Mill, and Bentham did not

write with modern medicine in mind. If Kant were to wander the sterile corridors and waiting rooms of a modern hospital, he might remind us that each patient is never a mere case or inconvenience: that each person, even at the brink of death, is not a biological mechanism but a bearer of intrinsic worth, an end in themselves whose life, and whose departure from it, should not be treated merely as an occasion for procedural utility or the quieting of professional consciences. Yet he might also recognise that our contemporary practices, the routine use of ventilators, life-support technologies, and long-term institutional care unsettles the neat distinction between the person as moral agent and the body as an object of intervention. Here Kant's insight endures, even as its limits become visible when dignity is understood too narrowly.

It is here that Henry David Thoreau comes into view. At first glance, he may seem a very unlikely presence in a discussion of healthcare ethics. He wrote nothing about modern medicine, assisted dying, or artificial intelligence. He was not a bioethicist, nor a moral theorist in any systematic sense. Yet, precisely in the face of modern healthcare's procedural and technological complexity, Thoreau's philosophical challenge, that moral life cannot be fully outsourced to laws, calculations, protocols, or even well-intentioned safeguards, acquires force. Where Kant offers principle, and Mill offers calculation, Thoreau draws attention to something less easily formalised: the irreducible demand of conscience, and the necessity of moral attention when rules and frameworks reach their limits.

However, this does not place conscience above law or render institutions irrelevant. Rather, it clarifies a boundary. Legal frameworks can define what is permitted; ethical theories can guide reasoning about harm and respect. But neither can fully discharge the responsibility borne by those who must act in particular situations of uncertainty, vulnerability, and consequence. In clinical settings, this becomes visible in moments when procedure has been followed, safeguards satisfied, and yet something remains morally unsettled.

Paul Ricœur makes a related observation.[3] Moral life, he suggests, cannot be reduced either to abstract principles or to fixed rules. General commitments, in respect for persons, or the aim of living well with and for others, must be worked out in particular situations where no rule fully determines what should be done. In such cases, what matters is judgement: the effort to respond to the situation at hand without losing sight of the values that guide it. Seen in this light, dignity is not something that can simply be applied, but something that must be interpreted and carried in practice.

Traditions often gathered under the name of care ethics draw attention to this reality. In different ways, Carol Gilligan and Joan Tronto[4] observe that moral life is not exhausted by principles or choices made in isolation, but is lived through relationships of dependence, attention, and responsibility. From this perspective, dignity is not a possession secured once and for all, but something that can be strained, supported, undermined, or restored through practices of care. It is enacted as much in how people attend to one another, with patience, restraint, and the quiet labour of sustaining another person's worth when they can no longer assert it themselves, as in the choices that are offered. Care, then, is not a threat to dignity but one of its primary expressions.

A similar insight appears in non-Western traditions. In many African philosophical accounts, often expressed through the idea of Ubuntu, dignity is understood not as an individual possession but as something realised in relationship: a person is a person through other persons. In this view, dependence does not diminish dignity but reveals the responsibilities that bind people to one another.

*

Anyone who has spent time in a hospital or nursing home knows how much dignity lives there: in the pace of a voice, in the space given for silence, in the decision to sit rather than stand over someone whose world has already narrowed. A monitor may continue to pulse long after conversation has fallen silent; clinicians hesitate between continuation and withdrawal, unsure whether intervention preserves life or merely postpones its end. In such moments, dignity is less a philosophical declaration than something disclosed in the uneasy balance between safeguarding life and acknowledging its limits.

At the bedside, this takes practical form: in how truth is spoken, in the pace of care, in whether attention is given or withheld. The sick person, even when stripped of strength, reason, or voice, remains an end in themselves. What changes is not dignity itself, but how responsibility is carried by those who must decide, interpret, and act in the absence of clear agency.

This can be seen both in its preservation and in its failure: in a nurse washing a body that no longer recognises itself, or in a curtain drawn too late; in a doctor repeating a prognosis because grief has silenced the first explanation, or in decisions made without a patient's understanding. Dignity, in this sense, is not simply present or absent, but unevenly enacted within the conditions of care.

In the modern hospital, how dignity is understood can be shaped by law, technology, and uncertainty. While policy can affirm autonomy and consent, practice can reveal hesitation, conflict, and limitation. What matters is not only what is decided, but how care is given, and whether, in the midst of constraint, the person is still recognised as more than a problem to be managed.

Illness, cognitive decline, and dependency are not aberrations from human life, but among its most predictable features. They are not simply medical conditions; they are moral conditions as well. They place people in relations of dependence that they did not choose and cannot easily escape. In such circumstances, dignity cannot simply be asserted; it must be recognised, protected, and sustained by others.

We might think of the man who cares for his wife through the slow erosion of her memory. There is nothing remarkable in what he does, nothing that would draw attention in any formal sense. He repeats the same answers each day, has learned to measure time differently, and has adjusted his life around the small, shifting needs of another. We do not hear him speak of dignity directly, yet it is present in the way he remains, in his refusal to turn away, and in the quiet persistence of his care when recognition itself has begun to fail.

It is in situations like this that the limits of autonomy become clear. We can clearly see how decisions are shaped by pain, fear, exhaustion, and unequal power, and many of the most consequential choices in healthcare are made under similar constraints. To describe them as fully autonomous is to misread the situation, for while autonomy remains important, it is no longer sufficient.

This helps explain why we tend to notice dignity most clearly when it is under threat. We do not notice it so much when things are going smoothly, but when something feels wrong: when treatment is prolonged without benefit, when bodies are sustained beyond meaningful life, when legal obligations collide with human grief, or when decisions must be made in uncertainty. Seen this way, dependence does not diminish dignity; it makes its relational character visible. When agency contracts, dignity does not disappear. What sharpens instead is responsibility, and the question of who must bear it.

At the bedside, dignity becomes visible less in declarations of independence than in the ordinary practices through which vulnerability is met without humiliation: the conversation repeated gently without irritation, the decision delayed until understanding returns. But if it is to guide action, it must first be recognised, and this recognition is rarely learned through formal instruction, but through encounter. A moment of being dismissed, even lightly, reveals how easily a person can be reduced; to be fully received, however briefly, shows what is at stake. Dignity, in this sense, is less a principle to be applied than a way of attending, visible in small acts: a question asked directly, the patience to wait for an answer, the decision to include rather than proceed without someone.

What threatens dignity in healthcare is seldom deliberate cruelty, but a failure of attention under pressure, when time is short, when systems take precedence, or when a person is described primarily in terms of condition, prognosis, or need. In such moments, care can begin to proceed around a person rather than with them. And decisions made 'in the patient's best interests' may still be experienced by the patient, or by those who care for them, as violations of dignity. We see examples of this reflected in law. In *McDonald v United Kingdom*,[5] the European Court of Human Rights considered the case of an elderly woman who, following the withdrawal of night-time care, was left to use incontinence pads despite not being incontinent. The Court held that this constituted an 'intolerable affront to her dignity,' recognising that even routine decisions about care can profoundly affect how a person is treated and understood. The case illustrates how dignity, in practice, is not only a matter of autonomy or consent, but of the conditions under which vulnerability is managed. To care with dignity, then, is not only to act in someone's best interests, but to remain alert to the limits of one's understanding, to recognise that the person before us exceeds any account we are able to give of them, even where voice, memory, or agency are diminished. Once recognised, dignity becomes harder to overlook.

*

In healthcare practice, dignity is often treated as a kind of status, associated with independence, self-command, cognitive clarity, and the ability to speak for oneself. Under this view, dignity appears to reside in performance, in maintaining control over body, emotion, and decision. When illness disrupts these capacities, dignity can seem fragile or lost.

However, a relational understanding resists this conclusion. Rather than something a person must sustain alone, dignity is recognised, upheld, and sometimes carried by others. Under conditions of vulnerability, it does not diminish; the responsibility to honour it intensifies.

The tension between these two perspectives is

rarely named, yet it shapes much of contemporary healthcare. A status-based account inclines institutions toward preserving function and defensible procedure; a relational account draws attention to lived experience, moral cost, and the meaning of continued intervention. When these orientations collide, dignity becomes a contested moral claim, invoked precisely where judgement is hardest.

This tension is also reflected in disability perspectives, which have long challenged the assumption that dignity depends on independence or cognitive capacity. From this view, the problem lies not in diminished ability itself, but in the conditions that render certain forms of life less visible, less supported, or less valued. Dignity is not lost when agency is limited; it is put at risk when care, recognition, and inclusion fail.

It is at this point that a further question arises, one that healthcare repeatedly encounters: when autonomy grows fragile, and choices must still be made, who speaks for dignity when the person at its centre can no longer speak with certainty for themselves? Someone must decide whether to continue, withdraw, intervene, or refrain.

Is it the patient, through prior wishes or an advance directive? Is it the family, through love and proximity? The clinician, through professional judgement? The court, through constitutional interpretation? Or the state, through law? Each may claim to act in the name of dignity, and each may be sincere. Yet their claims can conflict, and when they do, dignity risks becoming a rhetorical weapon rather than a shared moral concern. These tensions are not abstract. They emerge with particular force in cases such as *PP v HSE*, where competing claims about dignity collide in the absence of agency.

This difficulty is also visible in cases involving Jehovah's Witness patients who refuse blood transfusions. Here, the patient's wishes may be clearly expressed, yet their authority is not always accepted. In cases such as *JM v Board of Management of St Vincent's Hospital* and *Fitzpatrick v K(F)*,[6] Irish courts have intervened to authorise life-saving treatment despite refusal, either on the basis that capacity was lacking or that other interests, including the welfare of a child, took precedence.

These cases do not simply concern autonomy. They show how the question of who speaks for dignity is also mediated through judgements about capacity, welfare, and responsibility. The patient's voice is present, but it is not always decisive. Dignity, in this context, does not settle the issue; it is invoked on both sides of it.

A similar difficulty arises where the authority to

decide is itself contested. In *Glass v United Kingdom*,[7] clinicians administered treatment to a child against the wishes of his mother, without recourse to the courts. The European Court of Human Rights held that this amounted to a violation of the family's rights. What was at issue was not simply the clinical judgement, but the failure to recognise who was entitled to participate in the decision. Here too, dignity did not resolve the conflict; it lay in how that conflict was addressed.

*

There are also moments when the costs of dignity are not evenly borne. Families live with the aftermath of decisions; clinicians carry the moral residue of actions they felt compelled to take; institutions absorb risk by favouring defensible procedure; courts issue judgments that resolve legal questions while leaving ethical unease intact.

Speaking in the context of the constitutional constraints then in force, just before the news story about *PP v HSE* broke, the minister for health, Leo Varadkar, noted that such provisions could exert a 'chilling effect' on doctors, Further, 'Difficult decisions that should be made by women and their doctors, a couple or the next-of-kin where there is no capacity, and on the basis of best clinical practice, are now made on foot of legal advice. That isn't how it should be.'[8]

Dignity, in this sense, requires time, attention, moral labour, and sometimes restraint. It may sit uneasily beside compassion when intervention prolongs suffering, or beside restraint when inaction feels like abandonment. To invoke dignity without acknowledging these burdens risks hollowing it out.

There are many cases in which treatment continues long after its purpose has become uncertain. Few believe it will restore the patient to any meaningful life, yet no one wishes to be the one to stop. The notes are careful, the reviews regular, the language precise. Each step can be defended. Yet the effect, taken together, is a prolongation that feels less like care than hesitation. The patient does not speak. The family defers. The clinicians proceed. Nothing improper occurs. And yet, in the quiet accumulation of justified actions, something essential begins to recede: not life exactly, but the clarity about why it is being sustained.

In such moments, dependence does not diminish dignity; it exposes it. Those who remain at the bedside do not do so without cost. Clinicians encounter, repeatedly, situations in which what is required of them sits uneasily with what they believe ought to be done. This experience, often described as moral distress, may settle into what has been called moral residue, a lingering sense that something remains unresolved, even where the actions taken were justified.

Thinkers such as Hannah Arendt[9] warned of the moral risks that arise when human life is reduced to a biological process or an administrative category. That concern becomes acute in clinical settings, where life may be sustained long after agency and meaning have ebbed, and where the person risks being understood primarily through the terms by which they are managed.

The law has not been silent on these questions. In *Aintree University Hospitals NHS Foundation Trust v James*,[10] the UK Supreme Court made clear that decisions about treatment must be made in the patient's best interests, understood from the patient's own perspective, and with attention to the benefits and burdens of continued intervention. A treatment may prolong life, but it will not necessarily be a benefit. That judgement cannot be made in clinical terms alone. This does not remove the difficulty. It clarifies how decisions are to be approached, but not what they will be. Judgement remains, as does the possibility of disagreement about what those interests require.

Dignity is not something secured once and for all by appeal to principle or law – though law may protect it. It concerns how we treat people, particularly when they are least able to insist upon their own worth. In healthcare, this means recognising that moral work does not end when a form is signed, a safeguard satisfied, or a protocol followed. It begins again in what is done next, and in how those decisions are carried.

2

Assisted Suicide: Law, Language, and Conscience

Daniel Callahan once remarked that death itself appears to be 'in trouble,' and there is a sense in which this is true.[1] Modern medicine, that most humane and yet most ambiguous of human achievements, has given us the power to save lives, postpone death, and extend life with a thoroughness once unimaginable. We now survive illnesses that once killed swiftly. We are maintained, sustained, and preserved by technologies long after the body has ceased to cooperate with the will.

Yet whatever difficulties we may create for it, death remains the one appointment that none of us ultimately escape. The best we can hope for is a good death, neither furtive nor cruel, lonely nor stripped of meaning: to die peacefully, surrounded by loved ones, perhaps in one's own bed, at the close of a long, healthy, and fulfilling life.

For many, this hope is fulfilled quietly, even gratefully. But for others, illness arrives not as a closing chapter but as a prolonged siege. Advanced neurological conditions, such as motor neurone disease or multiple sclerosis, can leave the mind lucid while physical agency gradually diminishes. Pain is only one part of the ordeal; loss of independence, of speech, of privacy, and of control can weigh just as heavily. Some endure with extraordinary resolve. Others begin to question whether endurance alone defines dignity. Palliative care, however essential and humane, does not always answer the deeper anxiety: not merely how they will die, but who will decide when enough is enough.

There are some public questions that arrive not as arguments but as burdens, and assisted suicide is one of them. It presents one of the most searching moral questions of contemporary public life, carried into debate by lives marked by severe suffering, and by the experiences of those who have asked, in extremis, whether the law might recognise their wish to hasten death. Their appeals are not abstractions. They arise from fear, pain, the slow constriction of illness, and a desire not to be mastered by either. They draw us into questions where dignity, vulnerability, fear, and endurance meet in ways that resist simple judgement. Any serious reflection must begin there, in the reality of suffering.

*

There is a legal paradox shared by many jurisdictions, including the United Kingdom and Ireland. Suicide itself is not a criminal offence, decriminalised in England and Wales in 1961 and in Ireland in 1993,[2] yet assisting another person to end their life remains a serious criminal offence. In these jurisdictions, the dead face no sanction, but the living, those who help, those who accompany, those who love, may face prosecution.

This contradiction was brought into sharp relief in Ireland in the case of Marie Fleming in 2013,[3] whose legal challenge asked whether the law could recognise the predicament of a competent person trapped by physical limitation. Living with advanced multiple sclerosis, she remained fully competent, articulate, and resolute, yet was almost entirely immobilised. Physically incapable of ending her life herself, she required assistance. Marie Fleming did not ask for permission for others to end her life. Rather, she asked that her partner be permitted to assist her in doing what the law otherwise acknowledged, at least in the bare sense of non-criminality, as her own act. Yet because both euthanasia and assisted suicide remain criminal offences in Ireland, such assistance carried the threat of prosecution for the person she loved.

Her challenge was not theatrical; it was meticulous and restrained. She asked the courts to recognise that an absolute prohibition on assisted suicide violated her constitutional rights under Irish law and under the European Convention on Human Rights. In April 2013, the Supreme Court rejected her appeal, finding no constitutional right to die and affirming the State's interest in preserving life. She died eight months later, aged fifty-nine.

Similar tensions have appeared in the United Kingdom. Legal challenges brought by Diane Pretty,[4] Debbie Purdy,[5] and Tony Nicklinson[6] each exposed the limits of judicial intervention and failed to establish a right to assisted suicide. Courts acknowledged the gravity of individual suffering while repeatedly concluding that the question of legal change belongs ultimately to Parliament. The Assisted Dying Bill currently under consideration in the United Kingdom stands within this long and unresolved conversation.

A more recent case in Spain presents a related difficulty but in a different register. Noelia Castillo,[7] aged twenty-five, sought and obtained legal authorisation for euthanasia after a prolonged and contested process in which her capacity, psychiatric history, and the conditions in which her request arose were all subject to scrutiny. She subsequently died following that authorisation. In one sense, the system functioned as intended: safeguards were applied, objections were heard, criteria were tested, and a conclusion was reached. And yet the case does not settle. It gathers into a single life many of the tensions already present in these debates: suffering that is both physical and psychological; a will that is both asserted and questioned; a legal framework that operates as designed, and yet leaves something morally unresolved.

It would be possible to use such a case polemically, either as proof of the necessity of reform or as proof of its danger. But to do so would be to miss what is most difficult. Cases of this kind do not merely support positions already held; they expose the limits of the frameworks through which those positions are defended. They demand not only sympathy, but a form of attention capable of holding together all they contain: immediate suffering, certainly, but also the conditions in which suffering is lived, interpreted, and brought before the law.

Many other recognisable cases rarely reach the courts. An elderly person, at the end of a long illness, asks repeatedly, in the final days, to be allowed to go. These cases are resolved, if they can be called resolved, in hospital rooms where law provides the background but not the answer. The words come not as argument, but as insistence: 'Let me go.' Around the bed, adult children may stand divided. One may recall earlier wishes; another, perhaps guided by religious conviction, insists that life must be prolonged. Oxygen is continued. Fluids are maintained. Treatment proceeds, not because there is disagreement about the outcome, but because there is no agreement not only on what should be done, but whose understanding of duty prevails when love itself divides.

It is difficult to read about Noelia Castillo, Marie Fleming, Debbie Purdy, and others without feeling the heartbreak of their circumstances. Each of their pleas carries undeniable emotional force. Yet the law they challenged must speak not only to their suffering, but to the wider community in whose name it is written. The experiences that move us most are intimate; the law we are asked to frame is general. It cannot speak only to the exceptional case, and will shape the moral atmosphere in which all such cases are understood.

*

I find that clarity of language matters greatly in this debate, not least because confusion can quickly obscure the ethical questions at stake. Assisted suicide is generally understood as the act of deliberately providing assistance or encouragement to another person who then ends their own life.

In medical settings, the term 'physician-assisted dying' is used to describe circumstances in which a doctor provides a competent, voluntary patient with the means and instructions to self-administer life-ending medication themselves. This is generally distinct from euthanasia (from the Greek meaning 'good death'), defined as 'the act of deliberately ending a life to relieve suffering,'[8] which involves a more direct act by another person, typically a doctor, to end life with the intention of relieving suffering. However, even within that category, further distinctions are drawn between voluntary and non-voluntary, active and passive, each carrying its own moral and legal implications. Such taxonomies are not mere pedantry; rather, they reflect a very real underlying struggle to decide where responsibility lies and whether intention can ever be purified by compassion.

The term 'assisted dying' is less clear, and for that reason, perhaps more powerful. It has entered public debate as the preferred term in proposed legislation in the United Kingdom. Under the Terminally Ill Adults (End of Life) Bill, a Private Member's Bill currently before Parliament, it is worth noting that an act contemplated under that title would still involve a person ending their own life with assistance. But the choice of language is deliberate; the word 'dying' alters the tone in which the act is understood. It narrows the moral frame. 'Suicide' suggests interruption, decision, and agency, whereas 'dying' suggests a natural process already underway, inevitability and accompaniment. To choose one term over the other is to guide how the act is morally received. In other words, the act itself may not change, but the story we tell ourselves about it does. For law does more than permit actions; it shapes expectation, alters language, and gradually changes what a society understands by care, dependence, and worth. And stories, once legislated, do not remain on paper. They settle into conscience.

The UK Bill itself makes the architecture of the proposal plain. It defines eligibility in terms of adulthood, residence, and registration with a GP, and restricts access to those with a terminal illness understood as an 'inevitably progressive' condition with death reasonably expected within six months. Capacity is anchored in the Mental Capacity Act 2005, with an emphasis on a clear, settled, and informed wish, free from coercion. The mechanism remains one of assistance enabling self-administration, but eligibility is narrowed and framed within a medical and procedural structure. What is altered is not simply the criteria, but the description. Assisted dying, in this sense, is assisted suicide recast as a medical-legal response to terminal illness.

Viewed in isolation, the proposal appears tightly drawn. Yet the ethical question begins with what the law is willing to redescribe. Language in this field is not merely descriptive; it helps to shape the terms in which such acts are later understood and judged.

*

Of course, any discussion of assisted suicide must begin with the choices already available to those approaching the end of life.

In many jurisdictions, including the United Kingdom and Ireland, a competent adult may refuse medical treatment, even where that refusal will foreseeably result in death. Doctors may lawfully withdraw life-sustaining interventions, including ventilation, artificial nutrition, and hydration, where such treatment is refused by a competent patient or is no longer considered beneficial in accordance with the patient's wishes and best interests.

This principle, now well established in UK and Irish law, rests on the recognition that bodily integrity cannot be overridden simply because a life might be prolonged. For example, in *Re a Ward of Court*,[9] the Irish Supreme Court accepted that such a refusal might lead to what it termed a 'natural death,' and yet remained lawful. Subsequent decisions have reiterated the point in plainer terms: a competent adult is free to decline medical treatment, even where that choice appears unwise or grave in its consequences. English law has taken a similar course, most clearly in *Airedale NHS Trust v Bland*, where the withdrawal of life-sustaining treatment was held to be lawful in certain circumstances – specifically the case of Tony Bland, who had been left in a persistent vegetative state after the Hillsborough disaster. The House of Lords permitted the withdrawal of artificial nutrition and hydration because continued treatment was judged not to be in his best interests.[10]

What is striking is not the existence of this principle, but the kind of boundary it draws. The law permits a person to refuse life-sustaining care, knowing that death will follow, yet continues to prohibit assistance where death is more directly intended. The distinction is often explained in terms of intention, or of acts and omissions, though in practice it can appear less settled than the language suggests. What is clear is that the law has not remained indifferent to autonomy at the end of life.

It has recognised it, but only up to a point, and it is precisely the location of that point that remains contested within the courts, in medical practice, and in campaigns for assisted dying. The difficult question of justice arises where a person suffers profoundly, yet is not receiving any treatment that can be refused, and therefore has no lawful means of hastening death within existing frameworks. Should the law create a separate pathway for those cases, or does restraint serve a broader protective purpose that extends beyond individual vulnerable persons' circumstances?

Competent adults may also make advance directives in anticipation of future incapacity, specifying in advance what medical treatments they wish to refuse under particular circumstances. For example, do not resuscitate (DNR) orders entered into medical records allow patients to decline invasive interventions at the final threshold of life. These measures are now widely accepted as expressions of personal agency rather than as invitations to death.

Perhaps more contentious is the practice of palliative sedation. The steady improvement of palliative care and the spread of hospice services have undoubtedly transformed the experience of dying for many. Pain once considered inevitable can often be relieved, and hospice environments offer a form of accompaniment that resists the isolation often associated with terminal illness.

I had experience of this a couple of years ago while visiting a loved one in hospital. I remember sitting one evening in the room, the lighting low – a single candle had been lit – and beyond the window only the darkened silhouette of trees. Conversation moved in fragments. An elderly loved one lay slightly propped up against pillows. Their pain was managed with care; their agitation eased, and silence, when it came, was allowed to rest.

Thinking back, I remember no medical equipment competing for attention, no fluorescent glare, no sense of a struggle against the inevitable, and no atmosphere of heroic intervention. The nurse adjusted a pillow, checked a syringe driver, and stayed long enough for the quiet to feel companionable rather than awkward. What remained was attentiveness, pain measured and relieved, fears acknowledged without being amplified, and family members permitted to remain simply as family. We all knew death was approaching, but it did not feel like a defeat. And although we understood that death was plainly near, there was an absence of panic. The work being done there was not to defeat mortality but to soften its approach. And while it would be dishonest of me to pretend that fear vanished altogether at the time, I will say that something harsher had been removed: the sense that dying must be either a battle to be won or endured.

That experience, and others like it, matter because palliative care and assisted dying can sometimes be treated as if they answer one another. Yet they respond to different concerns: one to the relief of suffering through care, the other to whether some forms of suffering or loss of agency may be judged to be unendurable.

Indeed some, including John Keown, argue that the availability of effective palliative care substantially undermines the claim that assisted suicide is necessary, since much pain and distress can be relieved and dignity preserved without recourse to deliberate life-ending measures.[11] On this view, to introduce assisted suicide where such care exists is to abandon the more demanding moral labour of accompaniment.

A different view holds that palliative care, however essential, does not answer every form of suffering, particularly that rooted in loss of agency, prolonged dependence, or the fear of bodily decline. The debate, on this account, concerns not only the management of pain but the meaning of control, identity, and dignity at the end of life.

Both claims carry weight. Yet palliative care does not resolve every fear: it often becomes available only in the final stages of illness; not all suffering yields to symptom control; not all patients wish to trade pain for near-unconsciousness. And for some, the dread lies not in dying itself, but in the manner of living that precedes it. As Marie Fleming observed, the symptoms of pain may be controlled, but the prospect of being rendered barely aware of one's surroundings in order to remain alive was not, for her, a consolation. She stated that she lived with 'little or no dignity' and she was 'horrified at the thought of enduring months without being able to communicate, in pain and isolation, with full consciousness or being heavily sedated to the point of being barely conscious.'[12]

It has also been suggested that the legalisation of assisted suicide may, over time, alter priorities within care, subtly reshaping how death is understood in relation to suffering, when more should be done to provide palliative care, compassion, and understanding to those at the end of life to make the process of dying more comfortable. This concern has force, but it does not fully account for how such decisions arise in practice.

And then there is the controversial pragmatic argument that there is no moral difference between assisting in a competent terminally ill person's suicide and passive euthanasia,[13] where death is intentionally produced, either through the withholding or withdrawal of treatment, DNR orders, the 'doctrine of double effect', or by palliative sedation – all ethically accepted medical processes that happen all the time in a healthcare settings.

So why not legalise it? Surely assisted suicide as a way of accelerating the inevitable is more humane by ending suffering quicker?[14] Yet, this equivalence is rejected by many doctors, nurses, and palliative care specialists, since palliative sedation is not intended to end lives.

*

Despite the permissions already recognised in law, including treatment refusal, withdrawal of burdensome intervention, and palliative sedation, all of which may foresee death under certain conditions, the United Kingdom and Ireland both continue to prohibit assisted suicide. The line remains formally intact.

However, other jurisdictions have taken a different course. While their experience does not dictate domestic policy, it does illuminate what legal change may set in motion. Belgium, the Netherlands, Luxembourg, and Spain permit doctor-administered euthanasia in varying forms. Germany, Italy, and Austria allow assisted suicide. The UK, Ireland,

France, Cyprus, Malta, Portugal, and Slovenia continue to address the challenge of legislating for euthanasia or assisted dying.

Among the most persistent concerns raised by opponents of assisted suicide legalisation is the possibility of gradual expansion, often described as the 'slippery slope'. The concern is not that laws would change abruptly, but that practices introduced as exceptional may become ordinary over time. Legalising assisted suicide for a narrowly defined group may create momentum that is difficult to contain. What begins as a response to terminal illness may, over time, expand to include chronic conditions, psychological suffering, and, potentially, those whose autonomy is compromised.

There is also concern that should assisted suicide become normalised, then vulnerable individuals, such as those with disabilities, limited access to care, or diminished social support, may come to feel an obligation to choose death rather than impose upon others. Such influence need not be overt; it may operate through silence, exhaustion, or a culture that quietly ranks lives according to usefulness.

Belgium provides one of the most closely observed examples in this debate. Euthanasia was legalised there in 2002 under strictly defined conditions, but has evolved over time. In 2014, the law was extended to remove the age limit, permitting euthanasia for minors of any age under strict additional safeguards, becoming the first country to authorise euthanasia for terminally ill children under the age of twelve, and also beyond physical suffering to include psychological suffering.[15]

Official figures from Belgium's Federal Commission for the Control and Evaluation of Euthanasia record a rise from 236 cases in 2003 to 3,423 in 2023, now accounting for roughly 3 per cent of all deaths.[16] Some attribute this growth to demographic change, an ageing population, improved reporting, and clinical familiarity. Yet even on those terms, the scale of growth invites reflection. For, what was introduced as an exceptional response to extreme suffering has, over two decades, become a recognised feature of end-of-life practice. In Belgium, it has in some cases been followed by organ donation,[17] and a small number of patients now carry cards requesting that they not be euthanised, fearing that such requests may be too readily accepted and that alternatives may not be fully explored.

The Netherlands, with its longer history of regulated euthanasia, reports thousands of cases annually, accounting for over 5 per cent of national deaths in 2024, with ongoing debate about safeguards and categories as practice and public expectations evolve. Similar laws to those of Belgium exist in the Netherlands for children over twelve years.

Canada's Medical Assistance in Dying framework, introduced in 2016, now accounts for one in twenty deaths. In Quebec, it has also expanded through legislative amendment in relation to patients with Alzheimer's disease.[18] These developments are often presented as responses to particular cases, yet they suggest a certain movement in how such questions are approached, prompting similar discussion about limits.

Comparative experience has therefore become central to contemporary debate. These jurisdictions are not templates, but they do show how practices once regarded as exceptional or rare may become familiar and routinised. If we go back to the Belgium case, even where overall numbers in controversial categories, including cases of non-terminal illness, psychiatric conditions, and cognitive disorders such as dementia cases, conditions that can resist objective assessment, remain numerically small, this does not negate this concern. Their persistence and gradual increase, together with the later extension of the law to minors, which had been outside the law's original scope, illustrates the more incremental form of boundary movement. A steady state reached at a higher baseline, now encompassing a small but significant proportion of all deaths, may itself signal a profound cultural and medical shift of consequence.

Further, we must look beyond the numbers and categories, particularly to the socioeconomic context of the deaths, so that we do not dismiss unintended consequences. This point is sharpened by recent Belgian registry analysis, which identifies the absence of socioeconomic data as a limitation in understanding these cases.[19] It is not enough to know how many people died under the law, under what diagnosis, or whether the formal criteria were satisfied. We must understand what kind of life remained available to the person before death came to appear as a reasonable choice: whether there was adequate care, relief from pain, family or communal presence, financial security, and access to palliative support.

Where these things are absent, the moral meaning of a request to die becomes harder to read. It may be an act of autonomy; however, it may also be the voice of loneliness, fear, exhaustion, or neglect. A choice can be lawful without being wholly free. Dignity requires more than the recording of consent; it also requires us to ask what made consent seem necessary in the first place.

It is against this background that proposals for reform, including in the United Kingdom and Ireland, must now be read, since comparative experience suggests that interpretation continues beyond initial enactment; future boundaries are not fixed at the point of legislation and cannot therefore be fully predicted. Of course, none of this establishes inevitability, should assisted dying be legislated for in the United Kingdom or Ireland. But it does raise a quieter, more difficult question: how does law reshape moral expectations? Other countries show that practices once regarded as rare and extraordinary may slowly become normal. The issue is not simply numerical growth, though numbers matter; it is the gradual accommodation of conscience to what law has taught it to regard as ordinary, the normalisation of the unthinkable.

The point here is not inevitability but formation. Law does not merely permit acts; it teaches societies how to describe them, where to place moral emphasis, and what kinds of decisions come to seem thinkable, defensible, or even ordinary. The question will be not only whether safeguards appear sufficient at the moment of enactment, but how legal change may shape public understanding over time. Reclassifying assisted suicide as assisted dying would alter not only liability but description – and law, in describing, educates.

For this reason, the debate cannot be resolved by law alone. Legal frameworks define what is permitted, but not whether those permissions are ethically justified. Those who are asked to assist do not stand outside the act; they are drawn into it and must face the ethical and legal responsibility of deciding whether they should participate in what the law may regard as unlawful, and whether, under the weight of both law and conscience, what is being asked of them can be done at all. Therefore, the deeper question concerns what a society is willing to regard as care, what it is prepared to describe as mercy, and what obligations and responsibilities it continues to bear collectively.

*

Much of the practical debate in applied ethics rests on principlism, an approach that uses the framework proposed by Beauchamp and Childress,[20] who proposed four guiding principles: respect for autonomy, non-maleficence, beneficence, and justice. These principles have become a kind of moral shorthand in clinical settings, including debates about assisted suicide. Yet once invoked, they do not neatly settle the matter. They expose it.

Is there moral permission to choose death? Are there circumstances in which is it ever morally permissible, or even morally obligatory, to aid others in ending their lives? Should a society honour such requests, or does it have a duty to refuse them for the sake of the vulnerable? And if so, where does protection end and paternalism begin?

Perhaps the strongest case for assisted suicide rests on a person's right to autonomy: to determine the timing and manner of their own death, and to decide how much suffering is enough, particularly when their condition is unbearable and without prospect of improvement. There is real force in this claim. Yet autonomy is not exercised in a vacuum, and strength and vulnerability are not always opposites, but often entwined. Serious illness, intractable pain, and the prospect of profound physical or mental decline can bring fear, grief, a sense of diminishing worth, and a narrowing of horizons, all of which may shape judgement without extinguishing competence. The question remains whether a decision formed under such conditions can be fully described as autonomous. Yet it may be said, with equal force, that to deny such decisions is to substitute an external judgement for that of the person most directly affected, and to risk emptying autonomy of its meaning precisely where it matters most.

Moreover, respect for autonomy does not end with the individual. Decisions at the end of life inevitably involve others. In the United Kingdom and

Ireland, while suicide itself is not a crime, those who assist may face criminal liability. The burden of such decisions is therefore not borne by one person alone, but extends across families, clinicians, and the wider legal framework within which such acts take place. In 2015, Gail O'Rorke became the first person to be charged with assisting suicide in Ireland because she had assisted her friend, Bernadette Forde, who had multiple sclerosis and was wheelchair bound, by arranging travel to Dignitas in Zurich, Switzerland. Ms O'Rorke was initially charged with three counts under the Criminal Law (Suicide) Act 1993 but was found not guilty on two of the charges and acquitted of the third at Dublin's Circuit Criminal Court.[21]

Non-maleficence, the obligation to do no harm, is engaged by one of the oldest and most enduring objections to assisted suicide, an objection that arises not from theology or sentiment, but from the internal moral tradition of medicine itself. The long ethical tradition to which doctors are inducted, expressed in instruments such as the Hippocratic Oath,[22] the Declaration of Geneva,[23] the International Code of Medical Ethics,[24] the Statement of Marbella,[25] and later professional guidance, has long emphasised that the doctor's role is to preserve life and relieve suffering without becoming the direct agent of death, even when cure is no longer possible. To authorise doctors to provide the means of death would, on this view, alter that role, even if the final act remains with the patient. This does not mean, however, that medicine is obliged to prolong life at all costs. On the contrary, as we have already seen, modern medical ethics and law recognises the legitimacy of refusing disproportionate treatment and of prioritising comfort over intervention, even where death is foreseen.

Here, we may call on the principle of beneficence: acting in the patient's best interests, including the doctor's prima facie duty to relieve pain and suffering while attending carefully to the circumstances of each case. Yet medicine has traditionally resisted crossing the threshold at which the doctor becomes the agent, rather than the witness, of death. The concern is not merely symbolic. Once the healer is authorised to supply the means of dying, the moral identity of the profession is, on this view, altered. In contemporary debate, this concern is sometimes dismissed as antiquated or overly formal. Yet professions, like societies, are sustained by the limits they refuse to cross. To dissolve those limits is not necessarily to liberate, but to unmoor. For many doctors, legalisation risks altering the moral character of the doctor–patient relationship, introducing new forms of authority into moments already marked by vulnerability.

Uncertainty complicates matters further. Diagnosis and prognosis are rarely absolute, and capacity is not static; it can shift under the pressure of pain, fear, depression, exhaustion, and changing perspective. Even the most carefully designed safeguards, such as independent assessments, waiting periods, and second opinions, cannot eliminate subjectivity. Different doctors, shaped by their training, experience, temperament, and moral intuition, may reach different conclusions about the same patient.

Influence too may be present, and this need not be coercive to be effective. Family members may inadvertently communicate fatigue or distress without intending to do so.[26] Even the best-meaning clinicians, through accidental emphasis or omission, may frame options in ways that subtly steer decisions. Where life and death are concerned, such influences carry particular weight because even subtle pressure may affect an irreversible decision. This concern is reflected in *Vacco v Quill,* where the US Supreme Court recognised the common-law right to refuse unwanted treatment, but held that this did not extend to a constitutional right to assisted suicide, partly in light of the state's legitimate interest in protecting vulnerable people.[27]

And the variability does not end there. Some clinicians may be deeply reluctant to participate in assisted dying, while very different examples of Jack Kevorkian and Dr Wim Distelmans, in different legal and ethical contexts, illustrate how it is possible that others may be more willing to do so repeatedly. The concern here is that medicine may become uneven, dependent not only on the patient's condition, but on the disposition of those involved in their care.

At the heart of medical practice lies trust: the expectation that the doctor's role is to accompany the patient through illness, not to introduce death as a solution to suffering. Yet even the most conscientious clinician cannot entirely escape the authority of their position. Words spoken at the bedside carry a gravity unmatched in ordinary conversation. If assisted dying becomes one option among others, patients may begin to wonder whether recommendations are shaped solely by concern for their wellbeing, or also by institutional pressures, resource constraints, or broader cultural expectations about dependency and burden.

The danger is not overt coercion, but quiet alignment, or a narrowing of what appears possible. A suggestion, a tone, a hesitation, a family's fatigue, a patient's desire not to burden others: none amounts to force, yet each may shape what becomes thinkable.

The final principle, justice, presses the matter wider still. The question is not only what is owed to the individual before us, but what is owed to the community in whose name the law is written, to families, to medical professionals, and to those whose lives are already marked by dependence or precarity. At its most reductive, the utilitarian case for assisted suicide can appear straightforward: if suffering can be reduced, why should it not be? Yet such reasoning assumes more than it can safely know. It assumes that suffering can be measured, that the consequences of legal change can be contained, and that what is permitted for a few will remain bounded by the circumstances that first seemed to justify it. But once such judgements enter law and custom, they do not remain confined to theory. They begin to shape the way a society speaks about pain, burden, and the kinds of lives it is prepared to protect.

While the language of principles helps to organise the ethical terrain, it does not remove the underlying difficulty, which reappears again in different form within philosophical reflection.

*

Contemporary philosophical debate has produced sharply different conclusions.

Any discussion of assisted suicide inevitably

encounters the liberal tradition most clearly articulated by John Stuart Mill. In *On Liberty*, Mill offers a powerful defence of individual freedom, constrained only by the requirement that one's actions should not harm others. On this account, a competent adult is ordinarily the best judge of their own interests, and interference is justified only to prevent harm beyond the self.

It is not difficult to see why this framework has exerted such influence in contemporary medical ethics, particularly in end-of-life decision-making, where respect for autonomy has become a central organising principle. If a person, fully informed and free from coercion, judges that continued life entails suffering they can no longer accept, then the liberal argument suggests that the state should be slow to intervene. Yet even within Mill's framework, the question is not as straightforward as it first appears. The end of life is rarely a purely private matter. Decisions about dying are carried across relationships, family members, clinicians, and institutions, and their effects are seldom confined to the individual alone. Moreover, the conditions under which such decisions are made – pain, fear, dependence, and unequal power – complicate the idea of wholly self-regarding choice. So, while Mill's principle illuminates the moral importance of liberty, it does not go untested; perhaps it does not fully resolve the difficulty of how that liberty is to be understood, protected, and limited in circumstances where vulnerability is profound and responsibility shared.

Care ethicists such as Joan Tronto and Eva Kittay[28] begin from a different starting point. Rather than treating the individual as fundamentally self-sufficient, they emphasise the ordinary reality of human dependence and the moral significance of relationships. From this perspective, decisions such as assisted suicide may raise concerns that they can never be considered wholly self-regarding, because they arise within networks of care in which vulnerability is shared and responsibility cannot be neatly contained. To speak only of autonomy in such circumstances may risk overlooking how choices are shaped by fear, by the desire not to burden others, and by the quiet pressures that accompany illness and decline. What appears as an expression of freedom may, on closer examination, be inseparable from the conditions of dependence in which it is formed. The question, then, is not only whether a person is free to choose, but how that freedom is constituted, and who bears the moral weight of decisions made when independence has become fragile.

Margaret Battin and Peter Singer[29] have argued that respect for autonomy and the relief of intolerable suffering may justify assisted dying in carefully limited circumstances. Whereas, critics such as John Keown and Leon Kass respond that once medicine crosses the threshold of intentionally ending life, the moral architecture of care is fundamentally altered.

Ronald Dworkin's contribution remains especially important here, because he frames the issue not only in terms of liberty, but in terms of integrity. A person may judge that the manner of their death forms part of the meaning of the life they have lived, and that to deny them that authorship is to impose an ending alien to their deepest commitments. This gives philosophical depth to the appeal to autonomy, but it may also show its limits. For the question is not only whether a person chooses, but under what conditions a choice takes shape and what that choice is being asked to bear.

Again, Peter Singer's argument presses the moral force of suffering itself, and with it the intuition that to prolong agony simply because life continues biologically may itself be a form of harm.[30] This, too, has force, and any serious argument in this field must grant it while taking care to consider that suffering is rarely simply a datum, but can also at times be interpreted, mediated, and shaped by relationships, by fears of dependence, by social abandonment, by expectations about burden, and by the conditions under which care is made available or withheld.

From this angle, dignity cannot be reduced to preference or to the exercise of abstract autonomy. As Martha Nussbaum has suggested in another context, it is bound up with the capabilities and conditions that make a recognisably human life possible. Read in this light, a request to die cannot be understood apart from the situation in which it arises. A society that neglects care, tolerates isolation, or leaves persons to experience themselves as burdens may give rise to choices that appear autonomous, but whose conditions are less easy to accept without question.

Set alongside one another, these positions become especially instructive. Where one insists that suffering must be faced honestly; the other reminds us that suffering is lived within a social and political world that can itself fail persons long before death is requested. Between them, the question deepens: not simply whether death should be permitted, but what forms of life, care, and recognition have been sustained beforehand.

Deontological ethics, particularly in the Kantian tradition, resists this move. From that standpoint, suicide, assisted or otherwise, has often been understood to fail the test of universalisation.[31] To will one's own destruction as a solution to suffering is to treat one's rational agency as a means to an end, rather than as an end in itself. Whether or not one accepts this conclusion, it underscores a moral hesitation that cannot be dismissed as mere dogma. It asks whether there are acts that alter not only outcomes, but the moral terms in which we understand one another.

*

Hubert Butler warned against moral decisions made in abstraction from their historical consequences, and was wary of solutions that promised clarity at the cost of humility. The debate on assisted suicide seems to call for something of that caution. If law intervenes at the edge of life, it should do so with linguistic clarity and a certain historical humility. What is permitted may gradually become conceivable; what is conceivable may, in time, become customary. The discipline required may be less one of certainty than of attentiveness, to language, to conscience, and to the limits of what law can finally resolve.

Perhaps the question is not whether suffering can be eliminated, but whether we can remain alongside it without turning away, or deciding too quickly what mercy requires. The freedom to choose must include the freedom to remain alive. It may be a thin comfort that some tragedies remain beyond remedy, not as a failure of compassion, but as a reminder of its limits. There are certain dilemmas which the law, for all its authority, does not finally resolve. Assisted suicide may be one of them.

The cases that most move us arise from lives marked by forms of suffering most of us hope never to know. Their force lies in their particularity. Yet the law we are asked to frame must speak beyond the exceptional case to the ordinary moral landscape in which illness, dependence, and care unfold. To acknowledge this tension is not to diminish suffering, but to recognise that compassion alone cannot determine the boundaries of a general rule. The strongest cases do not settle the debate; they deepen it. They compel us to confront not only suffering, but the kinds of judgements we are willing to authorise in response, and the social world those judgements help to shape.

In the end, perhaps a society is revealed not only in the liberties it proclaims, but in the responsibilities it is prepared to carry: to accompany the dying without abandoning them to solitude, to protect the vulnerable without presuming their incapacity, and to resist, where it can, the temptation to resolve every tragedy through legislation. Whether assisted dying becomes law or remains prohibited, a deeper question may persist: not simply how we permit people to die, but how we understand the meaning of care when life approaches its end.

3

AI and the Moral Fabric of Medicine: Decision-Making, Responsibility, and Dignity

There are moments in history when a new technology does not merely change how we live but alters how we understand what it means to live at all. Artificial intelligence (AI) appears to be one of those moments. It arrives, almost unobtrusively, in the tools of our everyday life, in recommendations, diagnostics, and automated text. Yet its deepest implications lie elsewhere, in the fragile spaces where human existence is most exposed: at the hospital bedside where a monitor traces the slowing rhythm of a failing heart; the nursing-home corridor at dusk; the kitchen table where a prognosis is spoken gently between family members.

In such places, decisions must be made. How far should treatment continue? What suffering may be eased, and at what cost? And perhaps most difficult of all, who bears responsibility for what is decided?

As discussed previously, debates about assisted

suicide ask one version of that question: who should decide when life ought to end? AI introduces two more, perhaps more disquieting questions: what becomes of responsibility when decisions are no longer entirely human, but shared with systems whose reasoning we do not fully see? And what becomes of dignity when the person nearing death is increasingly encountered through prediction, categorisation, and digital mediation, rather than through the irreducibly human practices of presence, listening, and recognition?

*

One might begin, then, as the ancient philosophers often did, with mortality itself. Socrates spoke of philosophy as a preparation for death, a practice of examining life so carefully that its ending might be faced without illusion.[1] Centuries later, Marcus Aurelius returned to the thought that life is brief, and therefore not to be taken lightly.[2] To keep death in view was not an invitation to despair, but a way of seeing more clearly what is at stake in living at all.

Modern societies, however, have often tried to distance themselves from dying. Where death once tended to occur largely within homes and communities, it now frequently unfolds within institutions shaped by advanced medical technologies. Hospital monitors measure our vital signs, machines sustain breathing; decisions about how long treatment should continue and when it should stop are structured by clinical systems and legal frameworks governing consent, capacity, and best interests. Medicine has extended life in remarkable ways. It has also transformed dying into a technical event.

It may be that what we now call AI will represent the next stage in that transformation – not to replace care, but by reshaping the conditions in which it is given and the way decisions come to be made. The concern is that, in addition to the value it brings, responsibility may become distributed in ways that risk obscuring accountability and, more subtly, undermining dignity, unless its role remains carefully bounded by human judgement. These concerns are not only ethical but increasingly legal, as existing frameworks begin to adapt to decisions shaped by complex human–machine interactions.[3]

In what follows, the term AI is used primarily to refer to systems that inform or support clinical decision-making, particularly through prediction, pattern recognition, and data analysis, and the discussion focuses on a selection of the ethical and legal issues these systems raise, without attempting to provide an exhaustive account.

*

Computation has long been part of medicine, but its character is changing. Increasingly sophisticated systems now analyse vast collections of data, such as blood tests, imaging scans, and patient health records, identifying patterns that may elude even the most experienced doctor. In areas such as cancer screening, such systems are already used alongside radiologists to analyse medical images, helping to detect early signs of disease and allowing doctors to focus their time on the most complex cases.[4]

In some hospitals, predictive models already estimate mortality risk months in advance and identify patients who may benefit from early palliative-care referral based on subtle changes in clinical data.[5] In intensive care, experimental systems are being developed to support triage decisions by identifying patients less likely to benefit from aggressive treatment. Elsewhere, systems may alert clinicians when suffering increases, or when decline becomes more pronounced, while other technologies, including social robots and personal voice assistants, aim to alleviate loneliness among older patients, support remote monitoring, or organise complex medical information.[6] These developments are not speculative; they are emerging features of contemporary healthcare. Used well, particularly in systems where doctors and nurses are often stretched beyond capacity, they may offer genuine support.

There is something heartening in the idea that human intelligence, long strained against the limits of fatigue and fallibility, might now fashion for itself a patient and tireless companion. If AI can be taught to notice the faint early signs of disease, those whispers of danger that too often escape even the most conscientious eye, and act more precisely, then it represents not just a triumph of technology over humanity but a collaboration worthy of respect. Such tools could enlarge rather than diminish the doctor's vocation, freeing time and attention for the irreplaceable work of judgement, explanation, and care.

Yet the ethical and legal significance of such systems lies not only in their technical capabilities but in the kinds of decisions they may influence and in the relationships they reshape. Algorithms are beginning to extend clinical judgement beyond immediate observation, projecting possible futures in ways that reshape how decline is recognised and acted upon. In principle, this may help doctors to recognise when a patient is entering the final stages of illness earlier than before, potentially supporting the goals of palliative care by prioritising comfort and helping families prepare for loss. But prediction can introduce its own moral tensions. A number, once spoken, does not remain neutral. It enters the room as a quiet authority.

Suppose a system estimates that a person has only a small chance of survival. How should that information shape treatment decisions? Does such a prediction protect dignity by preparing us, or does it risk reducing a human life to a probability score?

This is one of the most acute dignity-related dangers in AI-assisted end-of-life care: the risk of the reduction of a person to a prognosis, where a life is interpreted primarily through what can be measured and predicted. The dying patient may come to be seen less as a person with memories, attachments, fears, and moral worth, and more as a cluster of variables generating a forecast. At the end of life, dignity lies in being recognised as a person with values, relationships, and meaning, not being reduced to a data profile or risk score.

Of course, medicine has always involved difficult judgements about prognosis and treatment: who is likely to benefit from intervention, and who is not; whether a treatment is initiated, continued, or withdrawn; and how to present options in conversations with patients and their families. But there is a difference between a doctor speaking with acknowledged uncertainty and a system presenting a numerical outcome. For the patient who hears such a prediction, the number is not merely information; it becomes part of the story they must now tell themselves about the future of their own life. They may hear it in a quiet room, in the presence of a doctor and family, but once spoken, it is difficult to set aside.

In some cases, such knowledge may also be very helpful, allowing patients and families to prepare more honestly for what lies ahead, and make space for conversations, decisions, and forms of care that might otherwise come too late. And yet, if communicated without sufficient care, such predictions may harden uncertainty into apparent fact, presenting probabilities as fixed outcomes, and making the person feel that their future has already been computationally settled before they have had space to interpret it in light of their own values. When a person's own account of what matters to them is silently crowded out, then statistically rational options can begin to displace morally meaningful ones. While they may appear to choose, they may in reality have been steered toward certain choices. The courts have, in a different context, already recognised this difficulty, suggesting that the communication of a prognosis cannot be treated as the neutral delivery of data, particularly where uncertainty may be heard as certainty.[7]

One might imagine, then, a patient, a retired teacher, perhaps, sitting in a hospital room as a doctor explains that a predictive model suggests a low likelihood of survival. The language is careful, compassionate. There is no sense of coercion. Yet the recommendation carries a certain quiet authority, as though it has been formed elsewhere and is now being relayed rather than discovered in the room. The patient is asked what he would prefer. He is invited to decide. And yet the conversation has already been shaped by what has been calculated. The range of what appears reasonable has narrowed, not by instruction, but by suggestion.

The difficulty is not only that a prognosis has been offered, but that it begins, subtly, to speak in advance of the person to whom it refers, risking a shift from recognising a life as it is lived to interpreting it as it is predicted. In such a situation, the legal requirement of informed consent is also placed under strain. The patient may agree, and sincerely so, yet still feel that the terms of that agreement were not entirely his own. When recommendations are shaped by poor communication, or complex or opaque systems, it becomes more difficult to ensure that patients genuinely understand the basis on which decisions about their care are made.

There are also concerns that AI may intensify

existing pressures around institutional priorities, such as efficiency, cost reduction, bed management, or throughput, which could quietly begin to shape end-of-life decisions, treating the patient as an operational problem rather than as a person approaching death.

Decisions of this kind are not new. Medicine has always had to confront limited resources and make difficult choices, balancing care for the individual suffering person before it with responsibility to unseen others, whether in emergency triage, organ allocation, or public health policy. AI does not create this ethical difficulty, but it may bring it into sharper focus and lend it a new form of authority.

The difficulty lies partly in how such systems are experienced. When AI predictions emerge from complex computational systems designed to identify statistical patterns across large populations, they may be remarkably effective at detecting correlations, but the path by which those predictions are produced can become less visible to those who rely on them. And numerically predicted recommendations appearing on a screen can carry a peculiar authority because they emerge from calculation rather than visible judgement, sometimes appearing more objective than the reasoning of individual doctors, even though their origins lie far beyond the bedside, and largely unseen, in software written by engineers, distant data gathered by institutions, and models approved by regulators. The doctor still stands before the patient, and the decision is still made in that encounter. But the conditions under which judgement is formed have changed.

What is at stake here is not entirely new. An earlier chapter considered the question of dignity in the context of assisted dying, and whether a life may be brought to an end under certain conditions. AI raises a prior question: how those conditions are identified, described, and understood in the first place.

A prognosis, a risk score, or a prediction may begin to shape what appears reasonable, what appears burdensome, and what appears to count as a life worth sustaining. In this way, the same dignity is at stake in both contexts, both in the moment of decision, and in the formation of the judgement on which that decision rests. But, if a person is increasingly encountered through what can be measured and predicted, there is a risk that the terms in which their life is understood begin to narrow before any explicit choice is made.

*

Precision can, in fact, sometimes mislead just as surely as inattention. We know this already. For example, a predictive model may estimate that a patient has only a small chance of surviving the next year based on patterns observed across thousands of similar cases. Yet medicine is filled with lives that exceed expectations: patients who recover when little improvement was thought possible, who persist beyond prognosis, who confound probability. Most of us have heard such stories. A cancer patient predicted to have only months to live responds to treatment and enters remission; another quietly regains strength when little improvement was expected.

These cases in no way invalidate statistical reasoning, but they do remind us of an older truth: that probability is not destiny. Between data and death stands a person who may not necessarily wish only to be predicted, but to be recognised with the wisdom of embodied human care. This point is not unlike the discipline developed from the Bolam test, central to *Bolitho v City and Hackney Health Authority*,[8] where judgement is not made safe merely because it is professionally accepted, technically supported, or widely relied upon; it must still be capable of withstanding logical scrutiny.

Nor is it far from the later insistence in *Montgomery v Lanarkshire Health Board*[9] that clinical judgement must attend not only to professional assessment, but to the particular patient and their circumstances, values, and choices. So too with AI, to preserve dignity is not only to avoid factual error. A prediction may be statistically impressive yet still be clinically inadequate or ethically troubling if it is allowed to eclipse the person whose life it purports to describe. Since courts have already recognised that expert authority must not be accepted uncritically, and that medical judgement must remain answerable to the patient before it, surely AI should not be exempt from that same discipline.

Concern has also been raised about the risk that care may be potentially displaced by technical optimisation. AI is oriented toward speed, efficiency, accuracy, and improved outcomes. Yet end-of-life care is not reducible to optimisation. It depends on empathy, presence, and trust, and concerns whether a person continues to be recognised as someone whose life has meaning beyond measurable outputs, whose worth does not diminish with frailty, dependence, age, or predicted mortality.

A system that improves efficiency while weakening compassionate interaction may still undermine dignity, even if it performs well in clinical terms. And the law has long recognised that clinical effectiveness is not the sole measure of care. As affirmed in *Montgomery v Lanarkshire Health Board*, patients are not passive subjects of medical expertise but individuals entitled to respect for autonomy and dignity. Likewise, in *Pretty v United Kingdom*, the European Court of Human Rights underscored that dignity forms part of the core values protected by law. A system may therefore succeed technically yet fail in what is most essential.

A perhaps subtler risk is that of moral distancing. This could potentially happen when decisions are supported by algorithmic recommendations, and clinicians may feel that responsibility is partially externalised. In this sense, AI can become a form of moral buffer felt against the burden of human responsibility, allowing difficult decisions to appear system-validated rather than personally owned. For the patient, this may amount to a form of abandonment precisely where dignified care requires moral presence. Yet dignity and law require that decisions affecting life and death remain attributable to accountable human agents.

There is a further consideration that is easily obscured by the apparent authority of AI systems: their safety. A model may perform well under controlled conditions and yet prove less reliable in the environments in which it is actually used. Clinical populations differ, data shifts over time, and systems trained on one set of assumptions may encounter another. What appears precise at the point of deployment may, under new conditions, begin quietly to falter.

This raises a question not only of performance but of responsibility. If a system's outputs change as its context changes – for example, if its accuracy degrades, or its recommendations begin to drift – who is expected to notice? The clinician at the bedside encounters only the result, not the conditions under which it was produced. Yet decisions continue to be made. The ethical difficulty here is not dramatic failure, but gradual misalignment. A system may continue to function, continue to produce recommendations, and yet no longer deserve the confidence placed in it.

At the end of life, where decisions are already finely balanced, such quiet shifts matter. They introduce a further layer of uncertainty into situations that are already ethically demanding, and they do so without necessarily making themselves visible.[10]

In an earlier chapter, I spoke of how Immanuel Kant famously argued that persons possess intrinsic worth and must never be treated merely as means to other ends, whether for efficiency or convenience. In medicine, this has often been taken to require that patients be regarded first and foremost as persons rather than as cases or statistics. A predictive model may be mathematically sound and yet morally incomplete. It may describe what is likely across many lives, but it cannot fully account for the unique trajectory of one, nor what dignity requires at the end of life: not merely the correct classification of risk, but the continued recognition of the person as someone who must never be treated as expendable or reducible to utility.

This tension becomes especially sharp when opaque systems are used to justify life-limiting decisions. If neither doctor nor family can adequately explain why a recommendation has been made, the patient may be subjected to a judgement that cannot be accounted for in recognisably human terms. Such opacity can diminish dignity by placing the person under the authority of reasons they cannot access. And it also raises legal concerns where decisions must be explained and justified, particularly if later subject to scrutiny in the courts or regulatory settings.

This difficulty is increasingly recognised in legal commentary on AI and evidence, and has begun to appear in litigation involving algorithmic or computerised decision-support tools. In *State v Loomis*,[11] a sentencing court's use of a proprietary algorithmic tool to assess a defendant's risk of reoffending, raised concerns about opacity because the method behind the score was protected as a trade secret. Loomis argued that he could not properly understand, test, or challenge how the assessment had been produced.

The issue has also arisen in medical litigation. In *Skounakis v Sotillo*,[12] a computerised weight-loss programme allegedly recommended a dangerous combination of medications, and the court admitted medical expert evidence as to whether that recommendation met the standard of care, underscoring that software-supported advice does not escape ordinary clinical scrutiny or responsibility. The duty of judgement remained with the doctor.

In healthcare, commentators have similarly warned that black-box AI may create evidentiary difficulties. If a system's reasoning cannot be explained, those affected may be unable to understand, test, or challenge the basis of the decision. The problem is therefore not merely technical but legal and evidential: a decision that cannot be explained risks becoming one that cannot be justified.[13]

*

Because AI now enters this delicate terrain as a powerful participant in medical decision-making, a further question arises. The more these systems shape clinical judgement, the more pressing it becomes to ask who ultimately bears responsibility for those decisions, and how the dignity of vulnerable persons can be preserved within increasingly complex technological systems of care.

As philosopher Luciano Floridi suggests, we now inhabit an 'infosphere', a world in which digital systems increasingly shape human decisions and relationships.[14] In such an environment, information itself becomes a form of moral power. At the edge of life, where medical decisions carry profound consequences, the use of such power must be approached with extraordinary care. AI, therefore, raises a deeper question about the distribution of responsibility within technological societies.

In traditional medical practice, responsibility is relatively clear. A doctor listens, evaluates the evidence, speaks with the patient and family, and recommends a course of action. A patient consents or refuses. Families participate. Institutions guide. The moral weight of the decision can be located, however imperfectly, within human relationships.

AI complicates that clarity. Decisions may now emerge from interactions between doctors, systems, data, and institutional protocols. Responsibility does not disappear, but it becomes more difficult to trace, and with it a certain clarity about who answers for what is done. This raises not only ethical but legal concerns, particularly where decisions must be explained, justified, and, if necessary, challenged.

This diffusion is not only a philosophical concern but a legal one. Should a decision emerge from interactions between humans and complex AI systems, where an algorithm contributes to a decision to withdraw treatment, for example, it becomes difficult to determine who is ultimately accountable for the consequences. Yet responsibility must remain somewhere. Is it with the clinician, the institution, or the system's designers?

Philosophy lecturer Andreas Matthias has described this phenomenon as a 'responsibility gap.'[15] If it becomes too diffuse, shared across systems, institutions, and individuals without true clarity, it risks becoming something that no one fully carries. The law has already encountered difficulty where responsibility is distributed across multiple actors, and recognised that duties in clinical contexts may extend beyond a single doctor–patient relationship, reflecting the interconnected nature of modern medical decision-making.[16]

Recent litigation further illustrates the difficulty. In *Sultzer v Intuitive Surgical, Inc.*,[17] a death following a robot-assisted procedure, allegedly involving device-related injury, raised questions not only about the surgeon's actions but also about the role of the system and its manufacturer. Such cases illustrate how AI and related technologies may make responsibility harder to locate.

Part of the difficulty lies in how such systems are governed. Ethical attention is often directed toward the moment of decision: whether a recommendation should be followed, and who is responsible if it is not. But the responsibilities surrounding AI extend well beyond that point. They begin in design, in the selection of data, in the assumptions embedded within models, and they continue through validation, deployment, and ongoing use.

But a system being approved for use is not the end of it. It must be monitored, questioned, and, where necessary, revised. Its performance must be observed over time, not assumed from initial success. In this sense, responsibility does not attach only to those who use such systems, but also to those who build, approve, and maintain them.

This enlarges the moral landscape. Responsibility is no longer confined to a single moment or a single decision. It becomes distributed across a sequence of actions, many of which remain distant from the bedside, yet nonetheless shape what occurs there.

This matters because medicine is not only technical, it is also moral. It is concerned not only with outcomes, but with how we recognise one another, and that recognition depends on attention. Decisions must be owned, explained, and, where necessary, defended, in terms that recognise the patient's dignity, not merely the system's performance metrics. Virginia Dignum has emphasised that such systems must remain embedded within accountable human institutions rather than replacing human judgement altogether.[18]

*

As Simone Weil observed, attention, the capacity to truly notice another person, is the rarest and purest form of generosity.[19] At the end of life, this form of attention becomes especially important. To attend to another person, to notice their suffering, fears, and hopes, is not merely an act of perception but an ethical act through which care becomes possible. It is rarely reducible to technical skill alone, nor can it be automated or reducible to data. It involves listening carefully to what may be said only indirectly: the patient who fears becoming a burden, the family member struggling to accept what is coming, the doctor trying to balance honesty with compassion. Any system that potentially weakens these forms of attention, even while improving efficiency, risks dehumanising the conditions of dying.

AI, of course, can excel at detecting patterns. Systems that monitor physiological signals may identify subtle changes in breathing, heart rate, or agitation that suggest distress, allowing caregivers to respond more quickly and precisely. Yet detection is not recognition. A system may register distress, but to recognise another human being as someone whose experience matters, someone whose life possesses dignity, is a fundamentally human gesture. Dignity is not preserved simply because distress has been accurately detected. It is preserved when suffering is received, interpreted, and answered within a relationship of care. Human life, after all, is profoundly dependent. Every person begins life in complete reliance on others, and many encounter similar dependence again in illness, frailty, or old age.

Joan Tronto and Eva Kittay have argued that dependence is not a failure of autonomy but a fundamental condition of human existence.[20] On this view, a person retains dignity not because they remain independent, but because they continue to be recognised, attended to, and cared for even when vulnerability makes independence impossible.

Perhaps this is one of the reasons that a patient may be continuously monitored and yet profoundly alone – if those systems quietly replace human presence rather than support it. Data may be gathered, analysed, and acted upon, and still something essential may be missing: bedside presence, conversation, and compassionate acknowledgement.

Care is not only the management of symptoms. It is the recognition of a person. This is one of the clearest dignity concerns in technologically mediated dying: that the patient is never ignored clinically, yet is nevertheless unseen existentially. In this sense, an ethical question may arise asking whether AI has the potential to alter the forms of attention through which human beings recognise one another.

*

The integration of AI may also complicate the legal standard of care. Doctors may increasingly be judged not only on their own professional judgement, but on how they engage with algorithmic recommendations, whether by relying on them too heavily or by disregarding them without adequate justification. In this way, AI does not merely assist care; it reshapes the expectations by which that judgement is evaluated. If AI alters the form that medical decision-making now takes, it also reshapes another part of the ethical landscape, raising questions not only about dignity but about autonomy and dependence.

The familiar framework of principlism – respect for autonomy, beneficence, non-maleficence, and justice – retains its relevance in the context of AI decision-making, but its application becomes more complex at the end of life. AI systems may appear to advance beneficence through improved prediction, or to support non-maleficence by reducing error. They may also seem to enhance autonomy by providing more information. Yet, as we have seen, these same systems have the potential to obscure understanding, complicate consent, shape decisions in ways that subtly crowd out that voice, and redistribute responsibility in ways that are not easily captured within the four principles alone. Justice, too, is placed under pressure where systems reproduce patterns drawn from unequal data.

Potential bias further complicates this landscape. AI systems trained on historical data may reproduce or amplify existing inequalities in healthcare. At the end of life, this raises the possibility that some lives may be implicitly valued less than others, undermining the principle that dignity is equal and unconditional. This risk is not merely theoretical: bias may arise throughout the AI development pipeline, including during data collection, labelling, model development, evaluation, and deployment.[21] This concern becomes more acute where systems trained on historical data potentially risk reproducing existing inequalities. One might imagine, for example, an older patient with multiple chronic conditions whose clinical record reflects years of complex illness and repeated admissions. A system trained on similar cases identifies a low likelihood of benefit from further intensive treatment. The recommendation is not presented as a judgement about the value of their life, but as a reflection of expected outcomes drawn from many others. Yet such data does not arrive untouched by history. Patterns drawn from past care may reflect not only clinical realities but also the ways in which certain groups, perhaps older patients, those with disabilities, or those from more deprived backgrounds, have historically received different levels of intervention. When such patterns are reproduced within predictive systems, they may quietly shape present decisions. No one intends to diminish the worth of the individual before them, but there is a risk of the patient's life being interpreted through a framework already conditioned by unequal histories of care.[22] The patient's projected future, derived from patterns in others, may begin to shape not only their treatment decisions but how far institutions are willing to sustain the costs of their care itself.

There is also a question concerning the data use. Medical information can be collected from lives lived in illness, vulnerability, and often dependence, and assembled into predictive systems to support care and shape how lives are interpreted. Privacy is a significant concern in the use of AI, and raises important legal questions, particularly under frameworks such as the General Data Protection Regulation (GDPR). Yet the complexity of such systems may distance individuals from whom it is drawn, from any meaningful sense of how it is used. A person nearing the end of life may become, in part, a source for future predictions about others. This may serve important purposes. Yet it also raises a question of authority of how that data is used to shape the care of others, and extends to whether the individuals, as data subjects, remain, in some sense, authors of their own experience, rather than becoming contributors to systems that speak in their place once they are gone.

Institutional pressures could further intensify this risk. Healthcare systems must manage limited resources, and AI tools designed to improve efficiency may encourage earlier treatment limitation or reduced intervention. In such cases, there is a danger that patients are treated as resource problems rather than as persons approaching death, raising serious concerns about both dignity and the legal defensibility of such decisions. If AI systems are trained on data shaped by structural inequality, they may encode lower expectations for the lives of older people, disabled people, people with dementia, or socially marginalised groups. In end-of-life care, such distortions are especially grave because they risk communicating that some lives count for less. Moreover, these concerns can sometimes extend beyond the clinical setting.

In recent years, concerns have been raised where insurers have used algorithmic systems to deny or limit care, sometimes at scale and with limited individual review. In other cases, AI-driven underwriting tools have been shown to encode socioeconomic bias, shaping access to coverage and pricing in ways that reflect historical inequality.[23]

*

AI may assist doctors and patients by analysing probabilities and outcomes, and in doing so may appear to expand autonomy by providing more information and supporting planning. Yet, as Shannon Vallor has warned, heavy reliance on automated judgement may produce a subtler effect: a gradual erosion of the human capacity to deliberate.[24]

Moral reasoning, like any human capacity, may weaken when too readily delegated. In clinical settings, this can take the form of automation bias, where doctors come to trust algorithmic recommendations too easily, particularly when they are presented with the appearance of statistical precision, even though their underlying reasoning may not be fully understood. Medicine already operates under pressures of time, limited resources, and institutional expectation. Technologies that promise clarity may therefore be welcomed precisely because they seem to reduce uncertainty, and the more reliable such systems appear, the harder they become to question.

Yet uncertainty is not always a defect. It is often the space in which judgement takes place, where dignity requires hesitation, humility, and sustained moral attention.

*

Finally, how AI enters clinical practice matters. It does not appear as something abstract, but through screens, prompts, and workflows that shape what is noticed, and when. A recommendation that is highlighted, timed in a particular way, or presented with apparent authority may carry more weight than its evidential basis alone would justify.

This makes design an ethical question, not only a technical one. A system that interrupts, that directs attention too forcefully, or that presents its conclusions as settled may narrow the space for judgement. One that is more carefully integrated may support it.

This also bears on trust. Patients and families do not encounter such systems directly, but through those who rely on them. A system may be accurate, and yet remain difficult to understand or question. In such cases, the issue is not only performance, but whether decisions remain recognisably human, and whether responsibility can still be seen to lie somewhere.

Between data and death stands a human life, and the task of accompanying that life with dignity, attention, and care remains irreducibly human.

Decisions about who lives and who dies, about who may be kept alive on machines or allowed to die in peace, are bound up with convictions about personhood, vulnerability, and dignity. Artificial intelligence cannot possess such convictions. It can only reflect, and sometimes magnify, those we bring to it.

The task is not to preserve decision-making in its previous form, but to ensure that responsibility does not become obscured within the systems we build. Where decisions are mediated, accountability must remain visible. Where judgement is supported, it must not be replaced. Where dignity is at stake, the patient must not become merely a data subject, a risk profile, or a node within an institutional workflow.

In the end, no algorithm stands beside the hospital bed. What remains is the presence of others: the hand held in recognition, a whispered story, a final apology, a blessing spoken softly, the quiet conversation in a dim corridor, and the family gathered around a kitchen table, trying to understand what comes next.

Conclusion

If one were, at this point, to recall the thinkers who have accompanied this discussion, figures who have written, in very different ways, about dignity, autonomy, responsibility, and the limits of human judgement, it is difficult to imagine that they would agree on very much. And there is no reason to suppose that they could be made to do so. Their disagreements are not incidental; they arise from fundamentally different understandings and views of what it means to be human, and of what is owed to one another in conditions of vulnerability and dependence.

What has changed is not their arguments, but the conditions in which those arguments must now be applied. Decisions that were once shaped more immediately by human presence are increasingly mediated by systems, medical, legal, and technological, that extend both our capacity to act and the range of considerations that bear upon action. At the same time, those decisions are made in conditions that are less stable than before: health services under strain, populations ageing, resources unevenly distributed, and circumstances in which questions of care are increasingly entangled with those of cost, sustainability, and resources.[1]

In this setting, neither assisted dying nor the use of artificial intelligence in clinical decision-making introduces entirely new ethical questions. Rather, they bring existing ones into sharper focus and reshape how they must be answered.

The use of artificial intelligence does not remove judgement from end-of-life decisions; it alters the conditions under which judgement is exercised. It may greatly assist, organise, or extend certain forms of reasoning, helping to identify and highlight relevant information, reduce certain kinds of error, and support more consistent and transparent decision-making. But it also introduces another layer between the person and the decision, one that carries its own authority. It potentially risks displacing attention by encouraging reliance on systems whose authority is not always examined, rendering responsibility less visible even as it remains fully in place. A life described primarily in terms of projection or probability may, over time, come to be seen in those terms, even where that is not intended.

Similarly, the legal framing of assisted dying does not resolve the moral difficulty at the end of life. It gives it form. It defines conditions, establishes safeguards, and seeks to contain what is permitted. Yet it also alters how such decisions are understood, and, over time, how they are expected.

Across these developments, agreement is unlikely. No solution emerges. But a shared concern may nevertheless be recognised, not as consensus, but as pressure.

It is whether, in extending our powers, through law, through medicine, and now through technology, we have also preserved the capacity to recognise what is being asked of us.

Not only how a life may end, but who remains answerable for that ending, and on what terms.

This is not a question that can be settled in advance. It cannot be resolved by principle, or by system, or by design. It remains, as it has always been, to be answered in the particular case, in the presence of another person, at the point where certainty gives way to judgement. And it is there, rather than in agreement, that the question of dignity at the end of life must finally be faced.

Notes

Introduction

1 O'Connor, Stephanie, 'Have we no more active rights over life, birth and death?', *The Irish Times* (11 August 2025).

2 Kets de Vries, Manfred F. R., 'Cancer in the public imagination: a psychological perspective', *Medium* (8 March 2026).

3 *Attorney General v X* [1992] 1 IR 1 (Supreme Court).

4 HIQA, *Investigation into the safety, quality and standards of services provided by the Health Service Executive to patients, including pregnant women, at risk of clinical deterioration, including those provided in University Hospital Galway, and as reflected in the care and treatment provided to Savita Halappanavar* (Dublin, 2013): https://www.hiqa.ie/sites/default/files/2017-01/Patient-Safety-Investigation-UHG.pdf.

5 *PP v Health Service Executive* [2014] IEHC 622.

6 Joint Committee on Assisted Dying (Ireland), *Report on Assisted Dying* (2024).

1. Dignity at the Edge of Life

1 Kant, Immanuel, *Groundwork of the Metaphysics of Morals*, trans. Mary Gregor (Cambridge, 1997).

2 Mill, John Stuart, *Utilitarianism* (London, 1863); Bentham, Jeremy, *An Introduction to the Principles of Morals and Legislation*, ed. J. H. Burns and H. L. A. Hart (Oxford, republished 1996).

3 Ricoeur, Paul, *Oneself as Another*, trans. Kathleen Blamey (Chicago, 1992).

4 Gilligan, Carol, *In a Different Voice: Psychological Theory and Women's Development* (Cambridge, MA, 1982); Tronto, Joan C., *Moral Boundaries: A Political Argument for an Ethic of Care* (New York, 1993).

5 *McDonald v United Kingdom* [2014] 60 EHRR 1.

6 *JM v Board of Management of St Vincent's Hospital* [2003] 1 IR 321; *Fitzpatrick v K(F)* (No.2) [2008] IEHC 104, [2009] 2 IR 7.

7 *Glass v United Kingdom* [2004] 39 EHRR 15.

8 Dáil Éireann debate vol. 810, no. 3 (11 July 2013): https://www.oireachtas.ie/en/debates/debate/dail/2013-07-11/13/.

9 Arendt, Hannah, *The Human Condition* (Chicago, 1958).

10 *Aintree University Hospitals NHS Foundation Trust v James* [2013] UKSC 67.

2. Assisted Suicide

1 Callahan, D., 'Is Death in Trouble? Chronic Conditions and End of Life Care', *The Hastings Centre for Bioethics* (2017).

2 Heath Service Executive (HSE) Euthanasia and assisted suicide; Criminal Law (Suicide) Act, 1993. Irish Statute Book.

3 *Fleming v Ireland & ors* [2013] IESC 19.

4 *Pretty v United Kingdom* [2002] ECHR 427. Dianne Pretty lost on appeal to the House of Lords as well as at the European Court of Human Rights at Strasbourg, however the Assisted Dying for the Terminally Ill Bill (Private Members Bill) was introduced to the House of Lords by Lord Joffe in 2003 and reintroduced in 2004. Lord Joffe stated, 'The Diane Pretty case highlighted the pressing need to allow terminally ill competent adults greater choice in the manner of their death.'

5 *R (Purdy) v DPP* [2009] UKHL 45. While the case did not change the law, the DPP issued guidelines in 2010 setting out public-interest factors to guide decisions on prosecution in cases of encouraging or assisting suicide.

6 *R (Nicklinson) v Ministry of Justice* [2014] UKSC 38. The Supreme Court of the United Kingdom considered the question of the right to die in English law of 'locked-in syndrome' sufferer Tony Nicklinson. The Supreme Court rejected the right to die a dignified death appeal.

7 Castillo, Noelia, euthanasia authorisation case (Spain, 2023), discussed in *El País* (2023) and related Spanish media reports.

8 National Health Service (NHS), Euthanasia and assisted suicide.

9 *Re a Ward Of Court* [1996] 2 IR 79.
10 *Airedale NHS Trust v Bland* [1993] AC 789 (House of Lords).
11 Jackson, Emily and Keown, John, *Debating Euthanasia* (Oxford, 2011); Young, R. 'Voluntary Euthanasia', *The Stanford Encyclopedia of Philosophy* (Fall 2016 Edition), Edward N. Zalta (ed.).
12 *Fleming v Ireland & Ors* [2013] IESC 19.
13 Dworkin et al. in 'Assisted Suicide: The Philosophers' Brief', *The New York Review of Books* (27 March 1997).
14 Paterson, Craig, *Assisted Suicide and Euthanasia: A Natural Law Ethics Approach* (Abingdon, 2008).
15 Aviv, R., 'Letter from Belgium: The Death Treatment', *The New Yorker* (22 June 2015); Cook, M., 'Another euthanasia scandal in Belgium', *BioEdge* (6 February 2016); Trott, R., 'Deaf Belgian twins end lives as they start going blind', BBC News (2012).
16 Federal Commission for the Control and Evaluation of Euthanasia (Belgium), Annual Reports (various years).
17 Wilkinson, D. and Savulescu, J., 'Should we allow organ donation euthanasia? Alternatives for maximizing the number and quality of organs for transplantation', *Bioethics* 26/1 (2012), 32–48; Report from 'Euthanasia and Assisted Suicide: Lessons from Belgium', conference hosted by the Anscombe Bioethics Centre, November 2014.
18 *Carter v Canada (Attorney General)* [2015] SCC 5.
19 Wels, J. and Hamarat, N., 'Trends in Assisted Dying among Patients with Psychiatric Disorders and

Dementia in Belgium: A Health Registry Study', *PLOS Medicine* 22/11 (2025).

20 Beauchamp, T. L., 'Methods and Principles in Biomedical Ethics', *Journal of Medical Ethics* 29/5 (2003), 269–74.

21 Hilliard, M., 'Gail O'Rorke found not guilty of helping friend take her own life', *The Irish Times* (2015). Judge McCartan stated that Ms O'Rorke's actions were 'too remote' from the suicide itself to legally constitute aiding and abetting and that the defence contended that Ms O'Rorke lacked any criminal intent in booking the tickets.

22 Edelstein, Ludwig, *The Hippocratic Oath: Text, Translation and Interpretation* (Baltimore, 1943): 'I will give no deadly medicine to anyone if asked, nor suggest any such counsel'. Not required by most modern medical schools.

23 World Medical Association, Declaration of Geneva (adopted 1948, last revised 2017): 'I will maintain the utmost respect for human life.'

24 World Medical Association, International Code of Medical Ethics (adopted 1949, last revised 2022): 'A physician shall always bear in mind the obligation to respect human life'.

25 World Medical Association, Statement of Marbella on Palliative Care (adopted 1992, revised 2011): 'PAS, like euthanasia, is unethical and must be condemned by the medical profession.'

26 New York State Department of Health Task Force on Life and the Law [press release]. Dept. of Health.
27 *Vacco v Quill* [1997] 521 US 793.
28 Kittay, Eva Feder, 'The Ethics of Care, Dependence, and Disability', *Ratio Juris* 24/1 (2011), pp. 49–58.
29 Battin, Margaret P., *Ending Life: Ethics and the Way We Die* (Oxford, 2005) and *The Least Worst Death: Essays in Bioethics on the End of Life* (Oxford, 1994), pp. 79–96; Glover, Jonathan, *Causing Death and Saving Lives*, 2nd ed. (London, 1990); Singer, P., *Practical Ethics*, 3rd ed. (Cambridge, 2011).
30 Singer, *Practical Ethics*.
31 Kant, Immanuel, and Mary J. Gregor, *Groundwork of the Metaphysics of Morals* (Cambridge, 1998).

3. AI and the Moral Fabric of Medicine

1 Plato, *Phaedo* (first printed 1513).
2 Marcus Aurelius, *Meditations*, trans. Gregory Hays (New York, 2002), bk 2, para 11.
3 Haden, C., 'The Consequences of the AI Act and Proposed AI Liability Directive on Medical Negligence: Will Physicians Fall Victim to "Red Tape" Rules?' *Oslo Law Review* 11/1 (2024), 1–9; Regulation (EU) 2024/1689 of the European Parliament and of the Council of 13 June 2024 laying down harmonised rules on artificial intelligence (Artificial Intelligence Act) [2024] OJ L 1689/1.
4 Cancer Research Institute, 'AI and Cancer: The Emerging Revolution' (14 January 2025).

5 Pinto, A., Santos, C., Aguiar, R., Oliveira, S., Cunha, D., 'The Use of Artificial Intelligence in Palliative Care Communication: A Narrative Review', *Cureus* 17/3 (13 March 2025).

6 Yang, Y., Wang, C., Xiang, X., An, R., 'AI Applications to Reduce Loneliness Among Older Adults: A Systematic Review of Effectiveness and Technologies', *Healthcare (Basel)* 13/5 (20 February 2025).

7 *Montgomery v Lanarkshire Health Board* [2015] UKSC 11.

8 *Bolitho v City and Hackney Health Authority* [1998] AC 232 (HL); [1997] 3 WLR 1151; [1997] 4 All ER 771; *Bolam v Friern Hospital Management Committee* [1957] 1 WLR 582.

9 *Montgomery v Lanarkshire Health Board* [2015] UKSC 11.

10 Mullainathan, S. and Obermeyer, Z., 'Does Machine Learning Automate Moral Hazard and Error?', *American Economic Review* 107/5 (May 2017); Obermeyer, Z., Powers, B., Vogeli, C., Mullainathan, S., 'Dissecting racial bias in an algorithm used to manage the health of populations', *Science* 366/6464 (25 Oct 2019), 447–53.

11 *State v Loomis*, 881 N.W.2d 749 (Wis. 2016).

12 *Skounakis v Sotillo* [2018] no. A-2403-15T2.

13 Citron, D. K., and Pasquale, F., 'The Scored Society: Due Process for Automated Predictions', *Washington Law Review* 89 (2014), 1.

14 Floridi, L., *The Fourth Revolution: How the Infosphere is Reshaping Human Reality* (Oxford, 2016).

15 Matthias, Andreas, 'The Responsibility Gap: Ascribing Responsibility for the Actions of Learning Automata', *Ethics and Information Technology* 6 (2004), 175–83.

16 *ABC v St George's Healthcare NHS Trust* [2020] EWHC 455 (QB).

17 *Sultzer v Intuitive Surgical Inc.* [2022] no. 9:24-cv-80137.

18 Dignum, Virginia, *Responsible Artificial Intelligence: How to Develop and Use AI in a Responsible Way* (Cham, 2019).

19 Weil, Simone, *Waiting on God*, trans. by Emma Craufurd (London, 1951).

20 Tronto, Joan C., *Moral Boundaries*; Kittay, Eva Feder, *Love's Labor: Essays on Women, Equality, and Dependency* (New York, 1999).

21 Cross, J. L., Choma, M. A., Onofrey, J. A., 'Bias in medical AI: Implications for clinical decision-making', *PLOS Digit Health* 3/11 (7 November 2024).

22 Ibid.

23 Mello, M. M., Rose, S., 'Denial—Artificial Intelligence Tools and Health Insurance Coverage Decisions', *JAMA Health Forum* 5/3 (2024).

24 Vallor, Shannon, *Technology and the Virtues: A Philosophical Guide to a Future Worth Wanting* (Oxford, 2016).

Conclusion

1 World Health Organization, 'Ageing and health' (Fact sheet, 1 October 2025).

Haus Curiosities

Inspired by the topical pamphlets of the interwar years, as well as by Einstein's advice to 'never lose a holy curiosity', Haus Curiosities are short works of opinion and analysis by notable figures. Haus Curiosities have been published since 2014 under the guidance of series editor Peter Hennessy and, since September 2019, with the assistance of contributing editor Ali M. Ansari. Welcoming contributions from a diverse pool of authors, the series aims to reinstate the concise and incisive booklet as a powerful strand of politico-literary life.

ALSO IN THIS SERIES

The Courage to Welcome: Between Principles and Pragmatism in International Affairs
Filippo Grandi, Catherine Ashton

Prophecy in Politics: Or, The Wigram Aspect
Kenneth Weisbrode

The Noble Army: The Modern Martyrs of Westminster Abbey
James Hawkey, Anthony Ball, Tricia Hillas, David Hoyle, David Stanton, Bashar Warda

Nonviolence: An Idea Whose Time Has Come
Ramin Jahanbegloo

Justice in Public Life
Claire Gilbert, Jane Sinclair, James Hawkey

Integrity in Public Life
Vernon White, Claire Gilbert, Jane Sinclair

Truth in Public Life
Vernon White, Stephen Lamport, Claire Gilbert

Trust in Public Life
Anna Rowlands, Claire Gilbert, Josie Rourke, Anthony Ball, James Hawkey

Art, Imagination and Public Service
Hughie O'Donoghue, Brenda Hale, James O'Donnell, Clare Moriarty, Micheal O'Siadhail, David Blunkett

Secret Service: National Security in an Age of Open Information
Jonathan Evans

The Responsibilities of Democracy
John Major, Nick Clegg

The Power of Politicians
Tessa Jowell, Frances D'Souza

The Power of Judges
David Neuberger, Peter Riddell

The Power of Civil Servants
Peter Hennessy, David Normington

The Power of Journalists
Nick Robinson, Gary Gibbon,
Barbara Speed, Charlie Beckett

Self and Society: Are Communal Solidarity and Individual Freedom Allies or Antagonists?
Michael Amherst, David Crane, Nick Inman,
Beninio McDonough Tranza, Tara McEvoy

Citizens of Everywhere: Searching for Identity in the Age of Brexit
Peter Gumbel

Explore the full Haus Curiosities collection: